IN DIVERSITATE UNITAS
Monsignor W. Onclin Chair 1997

KATHOLIEKE UNIVERSITEIT LEUVEN
Faculteit Kerkelijk Recht
Faculty of Canon Law

IN DIVERSITATE UNITAS

Monsignor W. Onclin Chair 1997

UITGEVERIJ PEETERS
LEUVEN
1997

C.I.P. Koninklijke Bibliotheek Albert I

ISBN 90-6831-919-1
D.1997/0602/28

© 1997 Uitgeverij Peeters, Bondgenotenlaan 153, B-3000 Leuven (Belgium)

INHOUDSTAFEL / TABLE OF CONTENTS

PRO PONTIFICE ET REGE

Laten we dit verhaal maar beginnen zoals we zijn: een beetje provincialistisch, levend als mens en arbeidend als canonist in het Koninkrijk België, anno 1997.

België is bij dit wat saaie plaatje een niet onbelangrijke component. Want hoewel sommigen zich afvragen of dit landje wel echt bestaat en nog meer of het zal blijven bestaan, was het in 1996 toch het decor voor allerlei spectaculaire gebeurtenissen die het wereldnieuws haalden. Alles nam een aanvang met de ontdekking dat de Waalse werkloze Marc Dutroux een aantal kinderen en jonge meisjes had gegijzeld, verkracht en vermoord. Meteen het startpunt voor een lange reeks onthullingen. Het gerechtelijk apparaat bleek te sputteren, politie en rijkswacht werden nu ook officieel onbetrouwbaar verklaard, politici vielen de een na de ander door de mand: nu eens bedwelmd door geldzucht, dan weer als pedofiel of ijverig participant aan schemerige roze balletten. Een witte mars met 300.000 deelnemers trok triomfantelijk door de straten van Brussel. Het systeem kraakte. De koning, namelijk Albert II, aan het bewind sinds 1993, was voor velen een laatste reddingsboei. Hij predikte een nieuw moreel bewustzijn en 90 % van de landgenoten waardeerde dat. Dat was België in 1996, afgezien van de gebruikelijke regenvlagen. Een mens heeft waarden nodig.

Allerlei geleerde en minder geleerde landgenoten becommentarieerden de gebeurtenissen, waaruit bleek dat velen het hadden zien aankomen, niet alleen tooghangers maar ook studiogasten in beschaafde televisieprogramma's. Daaronder geen canonisten, zelfs niet bij de minder geleerden, en terecht. Want voor een canonist overtreft wat er in het huidige België gebeurt wèl zijn meest stoutmoedige verbeelding, waarbij ik moet toegeven dat die verbeelding in zijn geval niet bar veel voorstelt. Maar toch.

Nog niet zo lang geleden, een tweetal jaar terug zeg maar, voelde de kerkjurist in België, en ook wel in een aantal andere Westerse landen, zich in het defensief gedrongen. De media richtten hun pijlen op een aantal in hun ogen archaïsch aandoende gebeurtenissen. Op 22 mei 1994 publiceerde de paus zijn brief *Ordinatio sacerdotalis* waarin te lezen

stond dat het tot de goddelijke ordening van de kerk behoorde dat vrou-
wen niet tot priester konden worden gewijd. Kardinaal Ratzinger
bestookte bisschoppen en gelovigen met instructies en brieven, onder
meer over de communie van echtgescheidenen. En begin 1995 werd
Mgr. Gaillot uit Evreux titulair bisschop van Parthenia.

Het was niet meer zo eenvoudig om canonist te zijn, althans voor wie
niet op zijn bureau bleef maar in plattelandszaaltjes, met hun formica
tafels en hun gevlamde beige tegels die bij de schoonmaak zo handig
zijn, over kerk en kerkstructuren lezingen geeft. "Vindt u ook niet dat de
kerk achterop loopt?", "Zoals de paus gezag uitoefent, is dát nog van
deze tijd?": zo luidden de vragen van doorgaans wat oudere, rustige,
goedwillende gelovigen. Ze monsterden daarbij zijdelings de dassen van
de spreker, de snit van zijn jasje: iemand die kerkelijk recht beoefent, in
deze tijd, daar zal ook wel wat mis mee zijn, iets dat zich uit in verou-
derde dasmotieven of de geur van mottenballen, zo kon men de vragen
in hun moede ogen raden.

Wie zoals ikzelf niet moedig is, noemde zich in die dagen nog wel
canonist - ontkennen helpt toch niet -, maar daarnaast in de eerste plaat
jurist. Dat was tenminste een eervol beroep, je werd er een beetje
salonfähig door of op zijn minst acceptabel in parochiezaaltjes. En dan
kon de lezing beginnen, over het onderwerp waar het bij de hedendaagse
canonist vrijwel altijd in een of andere vorm om gaat: hoe kan het god-
delijk recht worden verzoend met een minimum aan democratisch
gedachtengoed, aan transparantie of behoorlijke rechtsbescherming bijvoorbeeld? Er kon daarbij worden geput uit de rijke ervaring van allerlei profaanrechtelijke systemen, waar alles op wieltjes liep en de zorgen
hoogstens wat eenzame voetnoten vulden.

De canonist die zich jurist noemde: zo liep het tot 1996 aanbrak, de
sexuele en politieke schandalen het leven van de burger gingen beheersen en de media maandenlang in hun ban hielden. Op allerlei gebieden
van de maatschappij brokkelde het vertrouwen af. Onrechtvaardige rech-
ters en ongehoorzame wetgevers vertroebelden het geloof in het bestaan.
Men noemde zich nog node jurist, nog net, want ontkennen helpt ook
hier niet. Men bleef jurist, maar daarnaast toch op de eerste plaats canonist, want daardoor salonfähig en hartelijk welkom in parochiezaaltjes
met steeds weer die vloertegels, nu stilaan in een andere uitvoering, met
lichtere tinten onder meer.

In de media verloor de paus wat aandacht, en trad de koning op de voorgrond. Hij kwam op voor de zwakken in de samenleving, voor een nieuw moreel besef en voor het gezin als hoeksteen van de maatschappij. De koning spreekt onder de verantwoordelijkheid van de regering, is zelf politiek onverantwoordelijk en kan dus niet op zijn uitlatingen worden aangesproken. Een rechtgeaard canonist verwondert zich hierover niet. Men leze er bijvoorbeeld canon 333 § 3 op na: "Tegen een uitspraak of decreet van de Paus bestaat geen beroep of verhaal." Of canon 1404: "De Eerste Zetel wordt door niemand beoordeeld."

Maar hier houdt de vergelijking op. Terwijl het in onze samenleving nog steeds *de bon ton* blijft zich wat smalend over de paus uit te laten, is kritiek op de koning vrijwel onmogelijk geworden. Een beetje kritiek kan nog nét wanneer zij zeer technisch blijft, wanneer zij bijvoorbeeld de constitutionele rol van de koning scherp in het vizier poogt te krijgen. Maar wat ruimere kritiek, want meer inhoudelijke overwegingen, dat alles is nog toelaatbaar bij de borrel maar niet langer in de krant.

Vandaar de vraag: waarom de paus niet en de koning wel? Waarom aanvaardt de Belgische samenleving voor 90 % de koning, terwijl het aantal fans van de paus beduidend lager ligt? Is het een kwestie van persoonlijk charisma? Heeft het te maken met de inhoud van de boodschap? Zeer zeker niet. Zo is het moeilijk aan te nemen dat de inhoudelijke kwaliteit van het evangelie zou moeten buigen voor de vage en abstracte morele beschouwingen die de toespraken van koning Albert II kleuren.

Het verschil zit ergens anders, namelijk in de manier waarop paus en koning hun leiderschap inkleuren. Die loopt nogal uit elkaar.

De paus gedraagt zich als een **modern** leider, waarmee ik bedoel: modern in zijn leiderschap. Hij is iemand die zowel inhoudelijk als bestuurlijk een duidelijke koers vaart. Hij voert een alomvattend beleid, waar zowel inhoudelijke teksten als zeer concrete beslissingen zoals benoemingen of ontslagen van bisschoppen of sancties tegenover theologen mee gemoeid zijn. Het moderne leiderschap, dan men bijvoorbeeld ook in bedrijven terugvindt, houdt elementen van analyse en van besluitvorming in. Het op die manier gevoerde beleid, inclusief zijn heel concrete ingrepen en noodzakelijkerwijze soms minder prettige facetten, oogst niet altijd applaus. Het is bekend: grote verhalen behagen niet lan-

ger, misschien wel omdat ze altijd wat schaduwzijden vertonen. En keuzes doen pijn.

De koning daarentegen profileert zich niet als een modern, maar als
een **postmodern** leider. Juist omdat hij "slechts" een constitutioneel
monarch is, staat hij niet voor het hele beleid. Paradoxaal genoeg is zijn
gebrek aan reële macht in deze tijd een troefkaart. Hij wordt door het
concrete nimmer omkneld. Hij maakt kanttekeningen, plaatst vraag- en
uitroeptekens, maar heeft niet de ambitie het hele politieke leven te rege-
len of te controleren. In zijn betogen strooit hij nu eens een bloempje,
geeft dan weer een sneer. Hij legt de vinger op de wonde die hij verder
niet hoeft te genezen. Hij ontmaskert bestaande verhalen, zonder zelf
een compleet verhaal te vertellen, waardoor hij bij velen wellicht de al
bestaande indruk bevestigt dat die grote verhalen hebben afgedaan.
Indien de koning een concreet, alomvattend beleid zou mogen voeren of
pogen te voeren, zoals de paus dat doet, zou hij keuzes moeten maken,
voor verscheurende dilemma's komen te staan, op scepsis stuiten omdat
niet iedereen van elke concrete beslissing gelukkiger kan worden. Juist
door de greep te lossen, door niet echt te willen beheersen, door slechts
een positieve, bemoedigende rol te vervullen, gooit de koning hoge
ogen. De burger hoort liever een verhaal dat onvolledig is maar waarvan
de flarden aardig klinken dan een compleet verhaal dat precies daardoor
de tragiek van het eindige en beperkte leven niet kan verhullen. Hoe
minder verhaal, hoe meer schoonheid. Hoe meer flarden, hoe minder
dagelijkse zorg. De koning kan op een niveau blijven, waarop contradic-
ties, dilemma's en paradoxen achterwege blijven, of te abstract klinken
om echt pijn te doen. Een voorbeeld: de koning komt op voor solidari-
teit met de zwaksten aan de ene kant, en voor het gezin als hoeksteen
van de samenleving aan de andere kant. Maar wat betekent dat concreet
voor hen die precies tot de zwaksten behoren omdát hun gezinsleven
stuk is gegaan of omdat een harmonieus gezinsleven hun niet is gegeven
en nooit gegeven zal zijn? Heeft het leven zin zonder kans op een
gezin? Ik mag hopen van wel, waarbij hoop dan, meer dan een koninklijke, een christelijke deugd is.

Maar even terug ter zake. De paus stuit in onze samenleving op wan-
trouwen, omdat hij een modern leider is met een complete politiek, de
koning oogst waardering met een postmodern minimumprogramma van
liefde, sympathie en erbarmen, zonder verscheurende keuzes die hij zelf
moet maken. Betekent zulks nu dat de paus zich best ook maar deze

koninklijke stijl aanmeet, dat zijn leiderschap aan geloofwaardigheid zal winnen naarmate hij zich postmoderner opstelt? Is dát de politiek van de toekomst? Mijn antwoord luidt neen.

Neen dus, en wel hierom. Begin 1919 hield Max Weber in München een lezing over de "innerlijke roeping voor de wetenschap". Duitsland had net de eerste wereldoorlog verloren, na lange tijd uitzicht op winst te hebben gehad. Allerlei Duitse steden werden meegesleept door een revolutionaire koorts. Een paar weken nadat Weber zijn lezing ten gehore bracht, brak in München de burgeroorlog uit en werd een raden-republiek uitgeroepen. Bolsjewisme in Beieren, zoiets krijgt geen tweede kans meer, het lijkt wel een aanslag op het *ius divinum*. In die tijd van romantische politieke ideeën, van dromen die structuur moesten worden, hield de bleke en vermoeide Max Weber, voor een ademloos toeluisterend publiek, een pleidooi voor nuchterheid. Hij vertolkte de schitterende gedachte dat er aan de politiek te hoge eisen worden gesteld als ze wordt opgezadeld met de verwerkelijking van zin en geluk. Vroeg of laat volgt dan toch de ontnuchtering. Politiek schenkt géén zin, brengt niét het geluk. Zo vrees ik dat het ook een politiek zal vergaan die zich uitsluitend richt op die aspecten, elementen, bouwste-nen, kleuren, flarden die dit geluk lijken in de hand te werken of te ver-tolken. Of anders uitgedrukt: wie zin en geluk zoekt in woorden van een politiek leider, geeft wel aan dát hij dit geluk zoekt, maar hij zal het niet vinden wáár hij het zoekt. Van politiek mag wel een wat saaie con-sistentie worden verwacht, cohesie, rechtvaardigheid, maar geen flarden van hoop die het startpunt vormen voor het bereiken van een diep geluk. Laten we dus de politiek, sensu lato, niet overvragen, en niet hopen dat politieke leiders, verkozen of niet, politieke partijen, nieuw of oud, ons zouden brengen wat we zo graag willen maar zelf niet kun-nen vinden: geluk.

Maar geldt dit alles ook voor bestuur en beleid, voor leiderschap in de kerk? Dreigt ook daar het zuur van de nederlaag, wanneer meer wordt beoogd dan een behoorlijk bestuur? Moeten, anders uitgedrukt, zin en geluk elders worden gezocht dan in het canonieke recht? Natuurlijk zijn zin en geluk óók elders te vinden. De wereld zou het niet overleven, indien alle niet-canonisten ontroostbaar zouden zijn. Maar dat is uitein-delijk de vraag niet. Evenmin staat ter discussie of kerkrechtelijke arbeid de beoefenaar van het vak gelukkig kan maken. Natuurlijk wel, maar ook diepe droefenis is mogelijk. Wie zijn werk niet met hart en ziel doet,

geniet er niet van: dat is een algemene regel. En zonder incasseringsver-
mogen moet men geen canonist worden, nogal duidelijk.

Maar de echte vraag werd nog niet beantwoord: kan kerkelijk recht
ertoe bijdragen dat de mens zin vindt en geluk? Welnu, ik denk het wel.
Ik denk dat het mogelijk is, voor zover de canonist zijn werk niet te ver-
krampt opvat, voor zover hij zin en geluk niet ziet als een toegevoegde
waarde waarvoor hij hoogst persoonlijk zorg dient te dragen. Hij kan
wel de zoektocht naar zin en geluk stimuleren door erover te waken dat
canonieke structuren de glans en het mysterie van het geloof niet ver-
stikken in regels die knellender zijn dan nodig is. Kerkelijk recht moet
een kader zijn voor het geloof, zoals dat leeft binnen de kerk. Het brengt
structuur aan en tekent contouren, formuleert expliciet mogelijkheden en
trekt voorzichtig buigzame grenzen. Het is op zijn sterkst wanneer het
bijna onzichtbaar is maar toch helderheid en structuur schept zonder al
te vaak en al te veel pijn te doen. Maar wanneer het té ernstig wordt, kan
het ook dodelijk zijn. Ik zou zelfs durven zeggen: een canonist zonder
een licht gevoel voor ironie kan zijn taak wellicht niet aan. Die ironie
verraadt dan geen postmoderne afstandelijkheid en scepsis, maar juist
een grote betrokkenheid en het besef dat een al te bittere ernst wellicht
een mislukte poging zal inhouden om het geloof van zijn mysterie te
ontdoen.

Misschien is een probleem van het hedendaagse canoniek recht dat
er al te veel ernstige mensen mee bezig zijn. Let wel: ernstige mensen
zijn noodzakelijk, en zelfs vaak nogal vriendelijk, maar er moeten er
ook andere zijn. Canoniek recht is op dit moment vooral populair bij
mensen met een zeer uitgesproken binnenkerkelijke opstelling. De
meer behoudende strekking, met onder meer het *Opus Dei* heeft altijd,
terecht, veel aandacht aan grondige canonieke scholing geschonken en
aan het aanwenden van het kerkelijk recht ter ondersteuning van de
eigen theologische opties. Nieuw is, sinds enkele jaren, dat ook
progressieve katholieken zich steeds vaker op het canonieke recht
beroepen om hun, eveneens theologisch sterk geprononceerde, stand-
punten op het beleidsniveau te bepleiten. Ik denk daarbij aan de Euro-
pese Conferentie voor Mensenrechten in de Kerk, de Acht Mei Bewe-
ging in Nederland en de Vlaamse Werkgroep Mensenrechten in de
kerk hier bij ons. Nogmaals: ik vind dit alles uitstekend. Vele zeer
bekwame beoefenaars van ons vak hebben zo'n uitgesproken uitgangs-
punt.

Maar ik durf toch ook te pleiten voor een sterk middenveld van kerk-juristen, die misschien niet echt behoudend of niet razend progressief zijn, maar die met de nodige ironie tegenover hun eigen vak dat hoe dan ook erg klein is ten opzichte van het grote mysterie, toch dag na dag ijveren voor en werken met goede structuren voor een leefbare en geloofwaardige kerk. Evenmin als de politieke structuren, creëren de kerkstructuren zin of brengen zij geluk. Tot zover klopt de stelling van Max Weber ook met betrekking tot canoniek recht en bestuur. Maar anders dan de profane samenleving als dusdanig, heeft de kerk, via haar boodschap, wél de intentie zin en geluk te brengen. De kerk als dusda-nig, niet haar structuren, niet het kerkelijk recht dus, zoveel is duidelijk. Maar het is wel de taak van dat kerkelijk recht die zoektocht naar geluk en zin niet onmogelijk te maken. Kerkelijk recht geeft als dusdanig geen zin, maar het moet er zorg voor dragen die zin niet weg te nemen. En dat is al een zware dobber, in een milieu waar ondraaglijke ernst vaak het bestaan beheerst. Hoe krijg je, in de kerkelijke wereld, de gedachte aan-vaard dat te grote ernst ten aanzien van werken met kerkstructuren niet zelden wijst op een gebrek aan vertrouwen, op een **mentale** postmo-derne verbrokkeling die men precies daarom **structureel** wil bekampen, terwijl juist een iets ironischer aanpak van problemen die met canoniek recht te maken hebben, vaak getuigt van een rustig geloof dat zich niet moet optrekken aan de ernst van zijn structuren.

Valt deze stelling ernstig te nemen? En zo ja, mist ze dan precies daardoor niet een beetje ironie?

Prof. dr. Rik Torfs
Voorzitter facultcit kerkelijk recht

PRO PONTIFICE ET REGE

Let me begin my story as I am: frankly a little provincial, living and working as a canonist in the Kingdom of Belgium in the year 1997.

Belgium is far from being an insignificant component in this somewhat dull picture. While some people have been asking themselves whether this country of ours really exists and, more to the point, whether it will continue to exist in the future, 1996 saw it catapulted onto the world stage as the background of a medley of spectacular events. Everything started with the discovery that the unemployed Walloon, Marc Dutroux, had kidnapped, raped and murdered a number of children and young girls. We were immediately confronted with a whole series of revelations. The legal system appeared to falter, both local and national police were officially declared untrustworthy, one politician after another was forced to come clean: blinded by their lust for money, accused of being a pedophile or an enthusiastic participant in one or other unsavoury cover-up. The so-called 'White March' attracted 300,000 participants in a triumphant display of protest on the streets of Brussels. King Albert II, who had come to the throne only a few years earlier in 1993, became for many a final resort of appeal. The king preached a new moral awareness, and 90% of the population valued his words highly. Such was Belgium in 1996, to say nothing of the customary rain-squalls. People need values.

Learned and not-so-learned Belgians of every sort offered commentary on what had happened. It became evident that many had seen these events coming; not only the bar-stool citizens but also more than one studio guest on respected television programmes. Canonists, however, did not feature among the commentators, not even the not-so-learned commentators, and rightly so. For a canonist, the recent events which had taken place in Belgium were simply beyond imagination, and I feel obliged to add that in their case that imagination did not have a great deal to offer in the first place.

Not so long ago, say about two years back, the canon lawyers of Belgium, as well as those of a number of other Western countries, felt themselves forced onto the defensive. The media turned their cannons on a number of what they considered archaic sounding questions. On May 22, 1994, the pope published his letter *Ordinatio sacerdotalis* in which it was stated for all to see that it was part of the church's sacred order that women could not be ordained to the priesthood. Cardinal Ratzinger harassed bishops and faithful alike with instructions and letters, among them on the matter of communion for the divorced. At the beginning of 1995, Msgr. Gaillot from Evreux in France, became titular bishop of Parthenia.

Being a canonist was no longer a simple matter, at least for those who did not confine themselves to their desks but set about giving talks and readings on the church and church structures throughout the land in local community halls with their Formica tables and burnt-beige coloured tiles which are so easy to keep clean. "Don't you also think that the church is lagging behind?", "The way the pope exercises his authority! Is that still the way to do things in this day and age?": such was the kind of questions being asked by a well-intentioned, mostly older and somewhat composed representation of the faithful. In the meantime they inspected the speaker's tie and the cut of his jacket: someone who practices canon law these days must have some problem or other, one which might manifest itself in old fashioned ties and the smell of mothballs. Such thoughts became quite evident in their tired eyes.

Those like myself who lack a great deal of courage, did refer to themselves in those days as canonists – denying the facts does not help – but our primary term of self-reference tended to be *jurist*, civil lawyer. At least being a jurist was an honourable profession, providing one at the very least with a degree of acceptability in the parish halls of the country. Then it was time for the reading to begin, taking as its subject a topic which the contemporary canonist almost always has to deal with in one form or another: How can divine law be reconciled with a minimum of democratic expectation, transparency or the reasonable protection of one's rights? In response, the wealth of experience behind all sorts of secular legal systems – all of which appeared to run so smoothly and in which problems, at the most, constituted little more than isolated footnotes – offered themselves as source material.

The canonist who called himself a jurist! That is how it was until 1996 dawned and the emerging sexual and political scandals began to dominate the lives of Belgian citizens at every level, keeping the media in work for months on end. Confidence started to crumble at every level of society. Unjust judges and errant lawgivers clouded society's faith in its own existence. One still referred to oneself as a jurist, but only just, because denying the facts was not much help at this point either. One remained a jurist, but one's primary term of self-reference became canonist. At least canonists still had a level of respectability and were still welcome in those parish halls with their, now perhaps slightly different, floor tiles.

The pope was no longer the focus of media attention; the king had taken his place. He spoke out in support of the weakest members of the community, in favour of a new moral awareness and of the family as the corner-stone of society. The king speaks covered by the government, is himself without political responsibility and as such cannot be taken to task for what he has said. No rightly-disposed canonist would be surprised at such a fact. Take note, for example, of canon 333 paragraph 3: "There is neither appeal nor recourse against a decision or decree of the Roman Pontiff" or canon 1404: "The First See is judged by no one."

At this point, however, the similarity between pope and king ceases. While it continues to be *de rigueur* nowadays to speak somewhat slightingly of the pope, criticism of the king has become almost impossible. A little negativity is still acceptable if it is confined to technicalities, as, for example, when one endeavours to focus on the constitutional role of the king. Broader and more substantial criticism might still be permissible in the cafés but not in the papers.

We are confronted, therefore, with a question: why the king but not the pope? Why does 90% of Belgian society support and accept the king while the membership of the pope's fan club is diminishing fast? Is it a question of personal charisma? Has it to do with the content of the message? Clearly not ! It would be difficult to accept that the substantial quality of the gospel message ought to bow to the vague and abstract moral considerations which colour the speeches of King Albert II.

The true difference lies elsewhere, namely, in the manner in which pope and king nuance the exercise of their leadership. In this respect they differ quite distinctly.

The pope presents himself as a **modern** leader, by which I mean: modern in the way he exercises his leadership. He is a person who follows a particular course in both the content and administration of his leadership. His policies are all-embracing, not only in terms of the substance of his writings but also at the level of extremely concrete decisions such as the appointment or dismissal of bishops or the sanctioning of theologians. Modern leadership, as one can also find it exemplified in the business world, includes elements of analysis and decision making. A policy pursued in such a fashion, including its concrete interventions and, sometimes necessarily not-so-pleasant facets, does not always elicit applause. It is a well-known fact: grand narratives no longer satisfy, perhaps because they have always had their shadow side. Choices are painful.

The king, on the other hand, does not present himself as a modern but as a **postmodern** leader. Precisely because of the fact that he is 'only' a constitutional monarch, he does not represent policy in its entirety. Paradoxically enough, his lack of *real* power is something of a trump card at the present time. He is never restricted by the concrete. He might make notes in the margin, add question marks and exclamation marks, but it is never his ambition to organise or control political life as a whole. His arguments offer approval to one thing and disapproval to another. He might point at the wound but he is not required to heal it. He exposes existing narratives without offering a complete narrative in its place, thus confirming among many the already extant impression that such grand narratives are simply finished. Should the king pursue or attempt to pursue an all-inclusive policy as the pope does, then he would have to make choices, be confronted with heart-rending dilemmas, encounter scepticism in the fact that not everyone is made happier by every concrete decision. By the very fact of loosening his hold, by not really wanting to run the entire show, by confining himself to fulfilling a positive and encouraging role, the king stands a better chance of acceptance in the public eye. The ordinary citizen prefers to hear a narrative that is incomplete – the bits and pieces of which at least sound attractive – than a complete narrative which cannot conceal the tragedy of life's finality and limitedness. The less complete the narrative, the more attractive it appears. The more numerous the isolated fragments, the fewer the daily cares. The king can confine himself to a level on which the contradictions, dilemmas and paradoxes remain in abeyance or appear too abstract to really hurt. An example:

the king can offer his support to solidarity with the weakest, on the one hand, and to the family as the cornerstone of society on the other. What does such support mean in concrete terms, however, for those who find themselves among the weakest in society *because* their family life has fallen apart or because they have never known a harmonious family life and never will? Is life worth living without the chance of having a family? I would hope so; and my hope is more than 'royal' hope, it is a Christian value.

Let us return, however, to the matter at hand. In our contemporary society the pope has encountered mistrust because he is a modern leader with a complete 'policy' while the king harvests respect at every level with his postmodern minimalist programme of love, sympathy and compassion without himself having to make hard choices. Does that mean that the pope should take a leaf from the king's book and that his leadership will increase in credibility the more postmodern it becomes? Is that the politics of the future? My answer is No!

Why such a negative response? At the beginning of 1919, Max Weber gave a reading in Munich on the "interior call of the scientist". Germany had just lost World War I, having, for a long time, been in a winning position. German cities right and left were being swept along by a sort of revolutionary fever. A few weeks after Weber gave his talk civil war broke out in Munich and a soviet republic was proclaimed. Bolshevism in Bavaria ! Such a thing now would be unthinkable and comes across as an attack on the *ius divinum* itself. In a time of romantic political ideas, of dreams which cried out for structure, the pale and exhausted Max Weber appealed to his silent, attentive audience for sobriety. He expounded the quite brilliant idea that one expects too much of politics if one saddles it with the realisation of meaning and happiness. Sooner or later disillusionment has to follow. Politics does not offer meaning or bring happiness. Thus I fear that the kind of politics which focuses exclusively on those aspects, elements, building bricks, shades and scraps which appear to promote such happiness or make it real must also be doomed to failure. In other words, the person who seeks meaning and happiness in the words of a political leader might be stating that he is in search of such happiness, but he shall not find it where he is presently looking. One has the right to expect a certain, perhaps rather monotonous, consistency from politics, a degree of cohesion and justice but not the building blocks of hope which might lead to the achievement of profound happiness. Let us not ask too much of politics – *sensu lato* – nor expect that political leaders, elected or not, and political parties, new or old, can provide us with what we want but cannot find for ourselves: happiness.

Can all this be equally applied to church authority and policy, to church leadership? Are we not also under the same threat of failure if we expect more than reasonable administration? In other words, should we not seek meaning and happiness elsewhere than in canon law? Of course we should seek such things elsewhere. The world would not survive if all its non-canonists were doomed to be inconsolable. Ultimately, however, that is not the point, nor is it up for discussion whether the practice of canon law brings the canon lawyer happiness. Of course it does, but deep sorrow can also be its result. The person who does not give heart and soul to his or her work is not likely to enjoy it either; such is life. Likewise, if one lacks stamina, one should not become a canonist; that is pretty clear.

The real question still awaits our response: can canon law contribute to the meaning and happiness of human persons? In my opinion the answer has to be Yes! I think that it is possible to the extent that the canonist can avoid understanding his work in too contorted a fashion and to the extent that he does not consider meaning and happiness as a sort of appended value which he must attend to with the greatest personal concern. He can stimulate the search for meaning and happiness by making sure that canonical structures do not choke the lustre and mystery of faith with rules which are more restrictive than they need to be. Canon law ought to constitute a framework for faith, faith as it is lived within the church. It ought to provide structure and outline contours, formulate explicit possibilities and set careful, flexible boundaries. Canon law is at its best when it is almost invisible yet can still create structure and clarity without causing too much pain too often. When canon law becomes too serious, however, it also becomes deadly. I would even go so far as to say that a canonist who is not even slightly sensitive to irony is not up to the job. Such irony need not betray a postmodern aloofness or scepticism. On the contrary, it can imply profound involvement side by side with the awareness that an all too bitter seriousness might have its ultimate roots in an attempt to rob the faith of its mystery.

Perhaps one of the problems of contemporary canon law is that there seem to be far too many serious individuals engaged therein. Note well: serious people are necessary – and often even quite friendly – but other types are also essential. At the present time canon law appears to be popular primarily among those who have a very outspoken inner-church position. The more conservative tendency, including, among others, *Opus Dei*, has always and rightly set great store by a thorough canonical schooling and the appropriation of canon law in support of their particular theological options. New in recent years is the fact that more progressive Catholics have been appealing more and more to canon law as a source of support for their equally pronounced theological standpoints with respect to authority. The European Conference for Human Rights in the Church, the Eighth of May Movement in the Netherlands and the Flemish Work-group for Human Rights in the Church are but a few such organisations which come immediately to mind. I find all of this to be good news. Several highly competent practitioners of canon law have precisely such pronounced points of departure.

At the same time, however, I venture to appeal for an equally outspoken middle path among canon lawyers. While such individuals might not be extremely conservative nor impassioned progressives, they engage in their task as canon lawyers – small as that task might be with respect to the great mystery – striving for and working with good structures day after day in order to achieve a viable and credible church. Just as political structures are unable to create meaning or bring happiness, so it is with church structures. Up to this point Max Weber's position fits well with respect to canon law and church administration. In contrast to secular society as such, however, the church does have the intention – via her message – to bring meaning and happiness to her faithful. Clearly I speak here of the church as such, not her structures and not her canon law. Nevertheless, it remains the task of canon law not to make the search for happiness an impossible search. In itself canon law has no meaning but it has to ensure that it does not eradicate meaning altogether. That is not an easy task in a milieu in which unbearable seriousness often predominates. How is it possible within church circles to get across the notion that extreme seriousness with respect to working with church structures is not infrequently an indication of a lack of trust, of a postmodern mental disintegration which one wishes to control via structure while evidence of a little more irony in one's approach to the problems dealt with by canon law often gives witness to a serene faith which does not need to hold itself up by the seriousness of its structures?

Should this proposition be taken seriously? If so, does it not, for precisely that reason, lack a little irony?

Prof. Dr. Rik Torfs
Dean, Faculty of Canon Law

THE DIVINE AND THE HUMAN OF THE
IUS DIVINUM

The Problem

The doctrine of the *ius divinum* (*ius divinum positivum*, "promulgated" in the Revelation, and *ius divinum naturale*, "promulgated" in the reason of man - in contrast to *ius humanum/ius mere ecclesiasticum*)[1] has become a firmly established part of the *canonica traditio* (cfr. c. 6 § 2 CIC).[2] The character of it as a divine norm or law is seen in the assumption that these norms stem from God *ratione auctoritatis* as well as *ratione materiae*.[3]

The CIC/1983, as well as the CCEO, presuppose this very notion, whenever they refer to the category of *ius divinum* (without defining the term), although a wide variety of expressions is used, such as *ius divinum* (cc. 24 § 1; 1059, 1075 § 1 CIC), *lex divina* (c. 748 § 1 CIC), *ex divina institutione* (cc. 129 § 1; 207 § 1; 375 § 1 CIC; cc. 979 § 1; 323 § 2 CCEO), *ex divina ordinatione* (c. 113 § 1 CIC), *statuente Domino* (c. 330 CIC; c. 42 CCEO), or if a *ius proprium, ius exclusivum, ius nativum* is awarded to the Church (cc. 362; 1254 § 1; 1401 CIC; c. 1007 CCEO), or by connecting certain religious institutions with the Lord or His founding action or will (cc. 331; 840; 1055 § 1 CIC; 43; 776 § 2 CCEO).

---

[1] It should be realized that the term *ius divinum* does not originate from Canon Law, but from Roman Law: Cfr. BERGER, Art. Ius divinum, in: Paulys Real-Encyclopädie der classischen Altertumswissenschaft. Neue Bearbeitung X (1919) col. 1212-1215; WASER, Art. Fas, in: Paulys Real-Encyclopädie der classischen Altertumswissenschaft. Neue Bearbeitung VI (1909) col. 2001.

Referring to the notion of *ius divinum*: cfr. G. MICHIELS, Normae Generales Juris Canonici. Commentarius Libri I Codicis Juris Canonici I, Parisiis-Tornaci-Romae ²1949, 208-211; A. STIEGLER, Der kirchliche Rechtsbegriff. Elemente und Phasen seiner Erkenntnisgeschichte, München-Zürich 1958; A. STIEGLER, Art. Jus, in: LThK V (²1960) col. 1222 f.; K. RAHNER, Art. Recht, Göttliches R. u. menschliches R., in: LThK VIII (²1963) col. 1033; H. F. KÖCK, Grundsätzliches zur Geltung und Auslegung des Ius Divinum, in: H. W. KALUZA-H. F. KÖCK-H. SCHAMBECK (ed.), Glaube und Politik. Festschrift R. PRANTNER, Berlin 1991, 215-229.

[2] Cfr. H. PREE, Traditio canonica. La norma de interpretación del c. 6 § 2 del CIC, Ius Can 35 (1995) 423-446.

[3] Cfr. G. MICHIELS, Normae Generales (Note 1) 208-211; F. M. CAPPELLO, Summa iuris canonici in usum scholarum concinnata I, Romae ⁶1961, 9 f.

In spite of differing opinions[4] regarding the legal character of the *ius divinum*, and in spite of the fact that the justification and the significance of the *ius divinum positivum* on the one hand, and of the *ius divinum naturale*[5] on the other, is based on different arguments, the specific qualities of this kind of "law" can - according to traditional common sense on that topic - certainly be reduced to a more or less common denominator, as follows:

Immutability[6] and inderogability of the *ius divinum* (cfr. c. 1506 § 2 CCEO);

Invalidating force of the *ius divinum* in regard to all other (human) laws (cfr. c. 24 § 1 CIC);

Unlimited validity of the *ius divinum* in time and space (cfr. c. 8 § 1 CIC: ex natura rei illico ligent; c. 1489 § 1: ex natura rei statim obligant);

Indispensability of the *ius divinum* (cfr. c. 85 CIC; 1536 § 1 CCEO; cfr. also the expression *nulla humana potestate* in cc. 1057 § 1 and 1141 CIC; 817 § 2 and 853 CCEO).

---

[4] For an overview see: J. M. RIBAS-BRACONS, El derecho divino en el ordenamiento canónico, REDC 20 (1965) 267-320, 272-294.

One of the most famous authors who denied the legal character of the *ius divinum* was A. VAN HOVE; according to his opinion the matter of the *lex divina naturalis et positiva* together with the *lex aeterna* would belong to the Philosophy of law and Theology: A. VAN HOVE, De legibus ecclesiasticis, Mechliniae-Romae 1930, 81.

For new theses see: S. BERLINGÒ, La tipicità dell'ordinamento canonico (nel raffronto con gli altri ordinamenti e nell' "economia" del "diritto divino rivelato"), Ius Ecclesiae 1 (1989) 95-155; S. BERLINGÒ, Diritto divino e diritto umano nella Chiesa, Il Diritto Ecclesiastico 106 (1995) I, 35-65 and the bibliography listed in those articles; I. RIEDEL-SPANGENBERGER, Gottesrecht und Menschenrecht. Zur Legitimation, Limitation und Normierung positiven kirchlichen Rechts, in: H. J. F. REINHARDT (ed.), Theologie et Jus Canonicum. Festschrift H. HEINEMANN, Essen 1995, 99-109; H. PREE, Zur Wandelbarkeit und Unwandelbarkeit des Ius Divinum, in: H. J. F. REINHARDT (ed.), Theologie et Jus Canonicum. Festschrift H. HEINEMANN, Essen 1995, 111-135; A. HOLLERBACH, Art. Ius divinum. II. Kanonisches Recht, in: EvStLex I (³1987) col. 1414-1416; H. HEINEMANN, Art. Ius divinum, in: StLex III (⁷1987) col. 206-208.

[5] Cfr. O. HÖFFE-K. DEMMER-A. HOLLERBACH, Art. Naturrecht, in: StLex III (⁷1987) col. 1296-1318, 1302 and 1308; for an overview from a philosophical point of view see: E. WOLF-R. BRANDT-R. SPECHT-A. HÜGLI-R. RUZICKA-K. KÜHL, Art. Naturrecht, in: J. RITTER-K. GRÜNDER (ed.), Historisches Wörterbuch der Philosophie VI (1984) col. 560-623.

[6] "Das göttliche Recht ist unwandelbar, das menschliche Recht veränderlich": E. EICHMANN-K. MÖRSDORF, Lehrbuch des Kirchenrechts auf Grund des Codex Iuris Canonici I, München-Paderborn-Wien 1964, 4.

Further remarks on that issue: H. PREE, Wandelbarkeit (Note 4).

On the one hand we observe the severity of the consequences of this doctrine, for example in the impediments *iuris divini*. On the other hand, numerous cases of change, of development and even of abrogation or cancelling are very well known: some directives of the Bible have never been approved by the Church as *ius divinum*, notwithstanding the social (not only individual) impact of the matters such as the ban on swearing (Mt. 5,33-37), covering the head in worship (1 Cor. 11,1-16), the prohibition of lawsuits against brothers being settled by unbelievers (1 Cor. 6,1-11). The office in the Church is gradually developing together with the needs of the Christian communities; in the first decades of the life of the Church the communities were organized and led in many different ways. Without explicit embodiment in the Holy Scripture some institutions such as *iuris divini* came into existence only at a later time in history, for instance the hierarchy, the distinction between clergy and laymen, the papal primacy in its current shape, the Catholic Church and the Holy See as "moral persons" (cfr. c. 113 § 1 CIC).

In some cases legal norms, notwithstanding their former character such as *iuris divini*, were cancelled or at least essentially changed at a later time: for instance the prohibition of taking interest (Zinsverbot); the impediment of *mixta religio* according to c. 1060 CIC/1917 (cfr. cc. 1124 f. CIC); the explicit approval of religious freedom and of the freedom of conscience by Vatican II (DH) in direct contrast to the condemnation by the *magisterium* in the second half of the 19 th century.

Last but not least: in making a comparison between the CIC and the CCEO in regard to legal norms, which explicitly refer to the *ius divinum*, we notice that the CCEO in some significant regulations does not even have this norm, whereby the CIC on the same subject provides a norm *iuris divini*: e. g. cc. 113 § 1; 362; 375 § 1; 748 § 1; 1075 § 1; 1249; 1399; 1400 § 1, 1°; 1401.

In view of these facts the question arises about the origins and the true character of the *ius divinum*. The following reflections and suggestions are focused on the *hermeneutical* aspects of the question, dealing first and foremost with the *ius divinum positivum*. Two examples should point out and demonstrate the openness as well as the far-reaching consequences of the hermeneutical aspect - both on the practical and on the theoretical level (II). Part III contains the main thesis of this lecture regarding a new, but nevertheless fundamental question: the significance of the biblical hermeneutics for the process of eliciting and concretizing divine law; is there revealed law within the Holy Scripture - for instance in the unequivocal directive in regard to marriage and divorce? Part IV deals with the concept of concretization of the *ius divinum* and focuses on the necessity of this kind of transformation in view of the ontological structure of law as such. Finally, I will draw some conclusions and sum up a few consequences (V).

Two Examples of the Relevance and the Openness of the Question

The Significance of Dispensation

Although the norms of the *ius divinum* are regarded as indispensable, the church claims the power to dissolve (dispense) *vincula iuris naturalis ex voluntate humana orta*. As a rule, this power is applied to dissolving the bond of non-consummated marriage as well as in the cases of the *privilegium fidei* and for exemption from the obligations arising from vows and oaths. The possibility of these dispensations is based on the fact that in these cases the act of dispensation removes the object of the obligation. Thus, the basis of the obligation to God is abolished, so that the obligation itself ceases to exist. Under present Canon Law there is no consistent and homogeneous theory of dispensation, as can be made clear by comparing the possibilites of dispensation in the three cases of decisions for life (vows in a religious community; celibacy from holy orders; bond of marriage). The dispensation from vows is usually granted in a much easier and quicker way than the dispensation from the obligations arising from holy orders (except if the petitioner is a deacon). A dissolution of the bond of a *matrimonium ratum et consummatum* is not granted at all. Exactly what reason is sufficient to support the unequal treatment of the three cases?

It would be insufficient to warrant the unequal treatment by pointing out the character of the dispensation as a *gratia*, on the granting of which no one ever has an enforceable right since it is a matter of discretionary decision. Even the reason normally taken into account by the canonists in this context must be regarded as insufficient: i.e. the argument that a dispensation from vows does not really remove the obligation to God directly, but its basis and object, thus removing the obligation indirectly, as mentioned before; the dispensation from the obligation of celibacy resulting from holy orders means a dispensation from an obligation of a legal norm that is *iuris mere ecclesiastici* being dispensable by its very nature; but - in contrast - the dispensation from the obligations of the bond of a *matrimonium ratum et consummatum* is, right from the outset, regarded as impossible owing to the immediate binding force of the norm of indissolubility, which is assumed as *iuris divini*.

These explanations are not satisfactory because they do not deal with the problem in depth, not reaching the proper core of the problem, which lies in the meaning and significance of the *ius divinum*. Not even the traditional doctrine of the *potestas vicaria Ecclesiae*[7], which has been invoked for founding and legitimating the power to dissolve *vincula iuris naturalis ex voluntate humana orta* leads to the heart of the matter.

It is impossible to dissolve the moral bond resulting from a serious and valid commitment in any decision involving the whole person, all their life long, in the eyes of God. In each of the three aforementioned lifelong commitments insurmountable difficulties can arise, which exceed the moral strengths of the person affected, so that adhering to the decision in all its consequences would end in a personal disaster. In such cases the question arises: Does the church have the means, even in the case of the irreversible breakdown of a sacramental consummated marriage, to grant a kind of dispensation as an act of tolerance in order to enable the person to live a Christian life, in peace with God and with(in) the church?[8] Could the church not possess the power for reconciliation? If we presuppose that Jesus' words in regard to divorce rule out this possibility, we regard them as an immediately applicable legal norm - thus not taking into account that the word of God has to be taken as a whole, for example also the Good News of God's mercy.

---

[7] The traditional theory of the *potestas vicaria Ecclesiae* regarding it as a separate power, distinct from the other powers, cannot be maintained: On this topic U. NAVARRETE, Potestas vicaria Ecclesiae. Evolutio historica conceptus atque observationes attenta doctrina Concilii Vaticani II, PerRMCL 60 (1971) 415-486.

Interestingly the MP *De Episcoporum muneribus* (AAS 58 [1966] 467-472) speaks - explicitly referring to the *potestas vicaria* - about the Pope's power to dispense from *"leges divinae, cum naturales tum positivae"* (No. V).

[8] This question is posed by K. DEMMER, Moraltheologie und Kirchenrecht. Eine neue Allianz?, in: J. RÖMELT-B. HIDBER (ed.), In Christus zum Leben befreit. Festschrift B. HÄRING, Freiburg-Basel-Wien 1992, 352-366, 357-361.

What Canon Law Stands For

The significance of the doctrine of *ius divinum* for the legitimation of Canon Law, that means what it stands for and in which way it conceives itself, seems to be self-evident. I would like to demonstrate this with the help of a well known example, i.e. the teaching of the late Eugenio Corecco[9] as it was formulated in his last book *Il diritto della Chiesa*. I have chosen this clear-cut doctrinal position on purpose, because this way of conceiving Canon Law, as a fruit of the school of Klaus Mörsdorf, shows very distinctive features and has undoubtedly obtained a great deal of academic significance. Let me here make reference to only a few of the most important theses.

Corecco's teaching aims at differentiating his way of founding the Canon Law from the Protestant teaching of the *ius divinum*. According to the Protestant teaching, the *ius divinum* would belong to the *Ecclesia spiritualis*, while the *Ecclesia visibilis* would be ruled by the *ius humanum*. Thus the *ius divinum* would be conceived in a spiritualized manner, unable to have binding legal force within the visible Church, therefore being unable to create legally binding relations between the Christian faithful and the Church. According to this Protestant doctrine the *ius divinum* would determine only the relationship between the single *christifidelis* and God, a relationship only on the level of the individual conscience, but not on the level of the social relations within the *communio*.[10]

The disapproval of this kind of spiritualism on the one hand, and rejecting any kind of legal positivism on the other hand, is the reason why Corecco seems to regard the *ius divinum* itself as a legal norm with binding force. The legal structure of the Church is founded - according to Corecco - originally in the *ius divinum*, predominantly in the *ius divinum positivum*; the *ius divinum naturale* is only of secondary importance. The mystery of the Church does not consist of two separated elements, an inner, theological one and an external, juridical one. The dialogue between Canon Law on the one hand, and the Philosophy of Law and Theology of Law on the other hand, has only the purpose to help towards the discovery of the juridical dimension of Canon Law as a dimension being rooted within the elements of the economy of salvation, upon which Jesus Christ founded his Church. Therefore the

---

[9] E. CORECCO-L. GEROSA, Il diritto della Chiesa, Milano 1995.
[10] E. CORECCO-L. GEROSA, Diritto (Note 9) 3 f.

theological and the juridical characters of Canon Law are thereby connected with each other; thus a conflict between sacrament and law in the
Church is impossible right from the outset.[11]

According to this doctrine the *ius divinum* is *revealed law (diritto rivelato)*[12] in the proper sense of the word. Consequently, the *lex canonica*
is no longer regarded as *ordinatio rationis*[13], but as *ordinatio fidei*,
because it is a product of the faith only, not of the human *ratio*. In this
way the correct relationship between canonical norm and Catholic truth
is established.[14] Thus the binding force of Canon Law is, according
to Corecco, much stronger - in comparision with secular law -, since
Canon Law is rooted in the normativity of divine law itself, i.e. in the
Revelation.[15] For Corecco it would be "extrinsic" (*extrinsezistisch*, thus
referring to a dogmatic argument, which would need to be further discussed), to root the normativity of the *ius divinum*, that means its legal
character, not already in the divine elements, i.e. in the biblical directives, the word of God and the sacraments. Therefore the strange
methodological consequence of this doctrine: The science of Canon Law
is a *theological* discipline with a *theological* method.[16]

Thus Corecco docs not base the divine law on the grounds of the
concept of justice: for him, the objective of law is not justice, but *communio*.[17]

Although we have to take it as an indisputable fact that the legal
structure of the Church is essentially rooted in the *ius divinum*, I allow
myself to pose four questions in regard to the theological premises and
to the arguments proposed by E. Corecco.

Does a revealed law (*diritto rivelato*) in the proper sense of the word
indeed exist? What would it mean to implant the notion of law into the

[11] E. CORECCO-L. GEROSA, Diritto (Note 9) 5.
[12] E. CORECCO-L. GEROSA, Diritto (Note 9) 40.
[13] THOMAS AQUINAS, Summa Theologiae I/II, qu. 90 a. 4, uses this definition for laws
in general, not specifically for statutes of the Canon Law.
[14] E. CORECCO-L. GEROSA, Diritto (Note 9) 60-63.
[15] Cfr. M. WIJLENS, Theology and Canon Law. The Theories of Klaus Mörsdorf and
Eugenio Corecco, Lanham-New York-London 1992, 127.
[16] E. CORECCO-L. GEROSA, Diritto (Note 9) 57-60.
[17] E. CORECCO-L. GEROSA, Diritto (Note 9) 35 f.; WIJLENS, Theology (Note 15) 128-
130.

word of God? Can the word of God be understood - at least in some parts of it - in legal terms? Therefore:

I am afraid that Corecco's position leads to an even more spiritualized understanding of Canon Law than the rejected Protestant doctrine. The price Corecco has to pay for this kind of theologization of the Canon Law would be too high: the price of losing a well-defined notion of law with its own characteristic language and a special method - thus disregarding the fundamental option of legal certainty and even putting at stake the notion of law.

Could it be possible to derive Canon Law as such only from theological fundamentals? Of what importance are the other, non-theological principles, such as the formal principles of law, regarded as indispensable for the legitimation of any law?

Is it possible to distinguish *ius divinum* and *ius humanum* by a keen dividing-line, such as seems to be presupposed in Corecco's teaching?

The Dimension of the Divine in Canon Law: Revealed Law?

As far as canonists are dealing with the question of concretizing the *ius divinum* and with the nature of this, and its relationship to the *ius mere ecclesiasticum*, they usually do not take into consideration the proven results of the biblical exegesis - as far as I can see. A true interdisciplinary dialogue has not yet taken place. This is a really surprising fact, because the issue of the *ius divinum* means the way of making accessible God's will for salvation of man in the world of law and - in my opinion - this way has to take as its starting point the Revelation. The following reflections intend to plead that canonists in the future might not leave these sources unexploited. I am convinced that taking into consideration the structures of the inner-biblical hermeneutics would bear fruit for the process of cognition of *ius divinum*. Thus canonists could break new ground cooperating in an interdisciplinary manner with the scholars of biblical exegesis.

I will put the main focus deliberately on the Old Testament, especially pointing out the phenomenon of the Decalogue/Tora as a document summing up God's salvific will and its interpretations, reformulations and commentaries in the other scriptures of the Old Testament. Here lies a first and fundamental hermeneutical key for eliciting and interpreting the *ius divinum*. This hermeneutical key should be regarded as fundamental since - according to the *Theologumenon* of the essential *unity* of the two Testaments,[18] which is more and more underlined by exegetes as well as by official documents - we can no longer maintain our view of the Bible by exclusively focussing on the New Testament. Although in the person of Jesus Christ, the self interpretation of God has taken shape definitively, this new and definite Revelation did in no way abolish or overrule the Old (First) Testament; on the contrary, the Old Testament, as it was the Bible for Jesus himself, laid the basis for the New Testament, which has to be seen and interpreted in terms of the Old Testament, too (cfr. Mt 5,17-19).

With these prerequisites, taking into serious account the hermeneutics within the Old Testament is not to be considered just as an interesting, but definitively outdated completion, but - on the contrary - it has to be regarded as the indispensable school for the Christian hermeneutics in regard to the will of God.

The Decalogue itself is the result of centuries of literary formation and growth which can be understood as interpretation of the will of Jahwe.[19] As Georg Braulik expounds, the editing of the Decalogue ("Dekalogsredaktion") tied the many long-existing single laws and compilations of laws to general rules (the Commandments of the Decalogue), thus giving them an integrating centre, the Decalogue. "Die einzelnen Gesetze werden dadurch nicht auf eine Grundsatzregel reduziert, müssen aber jetzt im Kontext der ganzen Redaktion interpretiert werden. Umgekehrt konkretisiert und aktualisiert dieses ausdif-

---

[18] C. Dohmen, in: C. Dohmen-F. Mußner, Nur die halbe Wahrheit? Für die Einheit der ganzen Bibel, Freiburg-Basel-Wien 1993, 42: "Biblische Hermeneutik im Christentum muß immer vom 'Zeugnis der Schrift' ausgehen, und dies heißt, sie muß einsetzen beim Faktum der *einen* Heiligen Schrift in *zwei* Teilen, deren *erster* die Bibel Israels *als* Altes Testament und deren *zweiter* das Neue Testament ist."

Cfr. the principle formulated by AUGUSTINE: *"Novum Testamentum in Vetere latet, et in Novo Vetus patet"*, explicitly quoted by the Pontificial Biblical Commission in its document from April 23, 1993 (Sekretariat der deutschen Bischofskonferenz (ed.), Die Interpretation der Bibel in der Kirche. Ansprache Seiner Heiligkeit Johannes Paul II. und Dokument der Päpstlichen Bibelkommission, Bonn 1993, 91 [III. C. 1.]). In this context the document deals with the consequences for the exegesis of the inseparable unity of the Bible as a *"kanonisches Gesamtkorpus"*.

[19] The oldest legal element of the Decalogue is "die ursprüngliches Familienrecht zusammenfassende Reihe der Kurzprohibitive von Tötungs-, Ehebruchs- und Diebstahlsverbot ... mit dem Elterngebot": E. OTTO, Art. Dekalog: J. B. BAUER (ed.), Bibeltheologisches Wörterbuch, Graz-Wien-Köln ⁴1994, 103. Cfr. also the "Biographie des Dekalogs", in: F.-L. HOSSFELD, Der Dekalog. Seine späten Fassungen, die originale Komposition und seine Vorstufen, Freiburg/Schweiz-Göttingen 1982, 283 f.

ferenzierte Recht die Dekalogsgebote, was hermeneutisch für neue Situationen eine Fortschreibung geradezu fordert."[20]

Within the Old Testament the Decalogue is handed down twice: Ex 20,2-17 and Dtn 5,6-21. It is interesting to note that both editions ("*Redaktionen*") of the Decalogue are followed by genuine law books (Codes), which are concretizations of God's will summed up in the Decalogue: Ex 20,2-17 is followed by the "Bundesbuch" (Ex 20,22-23,33); Dtn 5,6-21 is followed by the deuteronomic law (Dtn 12-26).[21]

According to the well-founded results of the Old Testament exegesis, the differentiations between Decalogue on the one hand, and the other formulations of God's will on the other hand, were intentional and are of far reaching importance: Both kinds of formulations, the one being addressed directly to the people of Israel (Decalogue), the other one proclaimed by a mediator (Codes), are expressions of God's will.[22] The last ones are concretizations due to later changes of the circumstances bringing about new challenges. Therefore Norbert Lohfink distinguishes in the following way: God's will, in principle and immutable, is to be found in the Decalogue; its concretizing application, which is always changeable and adaptable according to the particular circumstances, is to be found in the Codes.[23] The Decalogue, also being a summary of God's will, must never be identified with it.[24] Another consequence resulting from the differentiation between Decalogue and the other formulations of God's will is the duty, "daß auch kommende Generationen vom gleichbleibenden

---

[20] G. BRAULIK, Die deuteronomischen Gesetze und der Dekalog. Studien zum Aufbau von Deuteronomium 12-26, Stuttgart 1991, 117.

In this context E. OTTO expounds: "Die Redaktionen im ... altisraelitischen Recht erfordern eine den einzelnen Rechtssatz übergreifende, den Kontext einbeziehende Interpretation der Rechtssätze." Cross references (mainly Ex 21,18-32 and 22,6-14) do not help to restrict the significance and the interpretation of the single legal norm to the facts of the cases immediately referred to. On the contrary, they lead to an interpretation of the single legal norm, "das den Rechtssatz als Teil des Ganzen einer Sammlung begreift": E. OTTO, Rechtsgeschichte der Redaktionen im Kodex Esnunna und im "Bundesbuch". Eine redaktionsgeschichtliche und rechtsvergleichende Studie zu altbabylonischen und altisraelitischen Rechtsüberlieferungen, Freiburg/Schweiz-Göttingen 1989, 181.

[21] L. SCHWIENHORST-SCHÖNBERGER, Das Bundesbuch (Ex 20,22-23,33). Studien zu seiner Entstehung und Theologie, Berlin-New York 1990, 412-414 and 417; G. BRAULIK, Gesetze (Note 20).

[22] N. LOHFINK, Kennt das Alte Testament einen Unterschied von "Gebot" und "Gesetz"? Zur bibeltheologischen Einstufung des Dekalogs, Jahrbuch für Biblische Theologie 4 (1989) 63-89, 86.

[23] N. LOHFINK, Gebot (Note 22) 87.

[24] N. LOHFINK, Gebot (Note 22) 87.

Grundwillen Gottes her neu nach der konkreten Formulierung des Gotteswillens für das Gottesvolk der eigenen Zeit fragen"[25]. The law concretizing the Decalogue remains changeable. It stands for the historicity of the realization of God's will, therefore requiring a continual reformulation.[26]

With regard to interpretation, the Decalogue must not be seperated from the laws interpreting it. This relationship between Decalogue and laws is also a characteristic of its time, "doch gibt es seither hermeneutisch kein Zurück mehr hinter das Prinzip einer solchen Verbindung von Dekalog und Einzelgesetzen als seinen Durchführungsbestimmungen"[27]. The Decalogue would draw its contents from the laws, thus being able to be a rule for everyone's life, not only at a legal level but also at a moral one.[28]

The lasting significance of the Decalogue lies in its intention and function to be a summary of God's will, which has been revealed to the people of Israel. All the other laws within the *pentateuch* are to be regarded as interpretations of the Decalogue.[29]

Within the hermeneutics of the Old Testament we also find the transition from moral directives on the one hand into legal norms on the other hand: The moral appeals at the end of the Decalogue (Commandments 7-10) show that the Decalogue in itself and as a whole is an ethical directive,[30] involving the whole person, thus including the essential

---

[25] N. LOHFINK, Gebot (Note 22) 87.

[26] N. LOHFINK, Gebot (Note 22) 89.

[27] G. BRAULIK, Gesetze (Note 20) 118.

[28] This is to be taken into consideration in the field of Theology of Law, if someone is dealing with this subject under the perspective of christian ethics, emphasizing the difference between the ethics of the two Testaments. A juxtaposition e.g. external, casuistic piety focussed on a literal implementation of law and a "*Leistungsdenken*" in contrast to internal ethics of charity nourished by grace is inappropriate. K. DEMMER describes the new ethos introduced by Jesus, as it can be found for example in the Sermon on the Mount, by saying, that according to Jesus in the New Testament the wicked is not only repelled/oppressed by resistance, but even overcome from the outset by the good. Jesus did not abolish the Old Testament law, but introduces a new "Verstehens- und Deuteschlüssel" and founds the Law anew - "Dem Jünger Jesu wird eine neue Kompetenz des Denkens und Handelns zugetraut. Er ist imstande, Verhängnisstrukturen der Geschichte heilend aufzubrechen.": K. DEMMER, Christliche Existenz unter dem Anspruch des Rechts. Ethische Bausteine der Rechtstheologie, Freiburg/Schweiz-Freiburg-Wien 1995, 129-134, 131 f.

[29] E. OTTO, Art. Dekalog (Note 19) 105.

[30] E. OTTO, Art. Dekalog (Note 19) 103.

values (virtues) and goods (protectable objects), but the Decalogue in itself is not a kind of law. The applicability on the level of the social order was brought about by legal norms concretizing the Decalogue.

An obvious example for values and goods, which are compulsory for any legal system, can be found in the regulations concerning human rights within the *Deuteronomium*: The right to life, to individual freedom, to an effective protection of rights, to personal property, to a just wage and social security, to freedom of marriage and protection of the family, to equality before the law, the *ius asyli*, the ban on slavery.[31]

To sum up, taking into account the hermeneutics within the Old Testament, we obtain at least the following insights into the idea of concretization of the *ius divinum*:

> the hermeneutics applied, helps to relate the inviolable and unassailable will of God on the one hand, to the necessary human concretizations and transformations on the other hand;

> in view of the relationship between Canon Law and theology, the hermeneutics within the Old Testament helps to clarify of what Canon Law stands for;

> it helps to uncover the theological dimension of any kind of law;
> the Old Testament teaches us to work on different levels of normativity, the level of the comprehensive moral demand regarding the person as a whole (e.g. in the Decalogue) as well as the levels of concretizations of God's will: These different kinds of normativity and the different levels of abstractness are used on purpose;

> God's will, as we find it for instance in the abstract summary of the Decalogue, in itself is not identical with its linguistic appearance and formulations. God's will underlies all other categories of human expression and levels of normativity, neither being a pure moral directive nor just a law. Therefore there is a great latitude for concretizing God's will available, which has to be made use of in the closest possible approximation to God's will (taken as a whole). Whereas God's will is unassailable, its concretizations made by man are always contingent and changeable and must take into consideration the needs of the individual case as well as the wholeness of God's salvific will.

[31] In detail on this topic: G. BRAULIK, Das Deuteronomium und die Menschenrechte, in: G. BRAULIK, Studien zur Theologie des Deuteronomiums, Stuttgart 1988, 301-323.

The Old Testament - as well as the New Testament - avoid both a fundamentalistic dealing with God's will (regarding for instance the Commandments of the Decalogue as immediately applicable rules of action, thus disregarding the peculiarity of the individual case), and any kind of relativism and Situation Ethics (disregarding the specific normativity of God's will, that means the biblical principles, values and goods). The Holy Scripture avoids both errors, because each level of concretization (the single laws in relation to the Decalogue; the decisions of individual cases in relation to the legal norms) remains rooted in and dependent on the supreme principles, i.e. the values and goods uncovering God's will, in the context of which the single norms must be interpreted.

Neither in the Old, nor in the New, Testament can the formulations expressing God's will be understood as legal norms. Jesus himself never enacted a law, not even in the most clear, valid and binding principles such as the claim for marital fidelity. This claim is in itself not a legal norm, although the probably earliest tradition Mt 5,32 is written in the formulation of a legal norm.[32] This might be the reason why this word of Jesus has been misunderstood and misinterpreted as directly applicable law for hundreds of years. According to the intention of Jesus this word certainly has to be regarded as a provocative prophetic appeal involving the whole person in its depth, deeper than any legal norm ever could.[33] Concretizing the biblical value into the shape of a matrimonial law is the task of the Church. Even within the New Testament the word of Jesus concerning marriage and divorce shows a variety of concretizations and adaptations in compliance with the particular circumstances (cfr. 1 Cor 7,10f.; Mk 10,11 f.; Lk 16,18; Mt 19,9). The history of the Catholic marriage law demonstrates a wide range of exceptions from the norm of indissolubility, thus concretizing the extent of this norm with all the possibilities of dissolving the bond of marriage, that we know very well. In the New Testament the example of the Pauline privilege as well as the reservation clause in Mt 5,32[34] confirm the existence of an inner-biblical hermeneutics of God's will concerning marriage. They must be regarded

[32] "But I say to you that every one who divorces his wife, except on the ground of unchastity, makes her an adulteress; and whoever marries a divorced woman commits adultery" (Mt 5,32).

[33] Cfr. G. LOHFINK, Jetzt verstehe ich die Bibel. Ein Sachbuch zur Formkritik, Stuttgart [10]1980, 138-143.

[34] U. LUZ, Das Evangelium nach Matthäus I, Zürich-Neukirchen-Vluyn 1985, 268-279.

as exemplary concretizations of God's will towards concrete situations and circumstances, having the character of a compromise in regard to the peculiarity of the situation, but without compromizing the will of God. The hermeneutical impact of these examples must be regarded as outstanding, demonstrating the necessity of concretization. Instead of it, Canon Law only transformed some of these Biblical messages into legal norms, such as 1 Cor 7,10f. (cfr. cc. 1143-1149 CIC) and Mt 5,32 (cfr. cc. 1151-1155 CIC); but the hermeneutical principle underlying these concretizations has not been made use of yet. The New Testament does not contain any immediately applicable legal norm, but the truth for the salvation of man - values, goods and principles, which need concretization for becoming applicable legal norms.

Selected Topics on Concretization

It is of course impossible here to develop an elaborate theory of concretization. It would be necessary to enlarge on the term "law" as such. Intentionally the concept only deals with selected references, which originate from the belief, that the taking into account of the biblical hermeneutics - in dialogue with the biblical science - is capable of enlivening the canonist's work.

According to the traditional doctrine - following with it the teachings of Thomas Aquinas[35] - human law is related to natural law in three different types of connection: *modus additionis, modus conclusionis* and the *modus determinationis.*

On the contrary, the *ius divinum* is predominantly looked upon as immediate, binding, superior law, which is enacted by Revelation and therefore does not need to be transformed in applicable law. Those canonists, who deny the legal character of the *ius divinum* regarding the divine and the human law as two separate orders, emphasize the necessity of "positivating" the *ius divinum* i.e. of a transformation into a legal norm of the canonical law, sometimes labeled as "formal reception" or as "canonisation". In the Italian and Spanish canonical science the terms "positivation" and "formalization" are widespread, and have been developed further by Salvatore Berlingò.[36] Hervada-Lombardìa in the recently edited '*Comentario exegetico al Código de Derecho canónico*'

---

[35] THOMAS AQUINAS, Summa Theologiae I/II qu. 91 a. 3; qu. 93 a. 3; qu. 94 a. 5; qu. 95 a. 2.

[36] S. BERLINGÒ, Tipicità (Note 4); S. BERLINGÒ, Diritto divino (Note 4); cfr. S. GHERRO, Principi di diritto costituzionale canonico, Torino 1992, 31-33.

hold the view of the legal character of the *ius divinum* and its need of "positivation". "Positivation" is neither understood as reception of divine law into the ecclesiastical legal order by an act of human authority nor as transformation into law, "sino su paso a la vigencia historica por la toma de conciencia ecclesial de su contenido concreto"[37].

A simple declaration by the *magisterium* or the perception by the *sensus fidei* suffices. On behalf of legal security and functional operability, the *ius divinum* furthermore, is subject to formalization. Without it, the *ius divinum* would remain only partially integrated within the legal order.

Beside the problematics of precise acquisition of the iridescent term of "positivity",[38] which has to assume a doctrine of "positivation", without going into the details of all these highly developed theses, the following questions in my opinion apply:

> Can the legal normativity be seen as the only one to guarantee the unity of Canon Law? The unifying function of the *ius divinum* - in my opinion - does not presuppose the legal character of the *ius divinum*.

> Is the fact that the divine prescript *per se* is not a legal clause, sufficiently considered - even if contents of that kind are capable of being transformed into law as the Old Testament shows?

> Does the cognition/notice of contents of the *ius divinum* by itself suffice in order to make it binding as law within the Church? Isn't the meaning of the authoritative component in enacting a norm of the *ius divinum* underestimated, since the qualification as law is an additional step in relation to the perception of this truth itself, which underlies the contents of the legal norm? This step, however, presupposes acts of selection and legal formulation on the human lawgiver side, because not all contents of the divine truth can and must be transformed into law. Especially, not every ethical value is capable of being transformed into a legal norm, since it is not the duty of law to make morality enforceable.[39]

> Does this doctrine pay sufficient attention to the structure of law? The notion of law cannot be applied in an equal manner on both the supreme principles and the concrete applicable legal norms.

[37] J. HERVADA-P. LOMBARDÍA, Prolegómenos I. Introducción al Derecho Canónico, in: A. MARZOA-J. MIRAS-R. RODRIGUEZ-OCAÑA, Comentario exegético al Código de Derecho Canónico I, Pamplona 1996, 33-155, 50-55.

[38] Cfr. J.-G. BLÜHDORN-C. JAMME, Art. Positiv, Positivität, in: J. RITTER-K. GRÜNDER (ed.), Historisches Wörterbuch der Philosophie VII (1989) col. 1106-1118.

[39] Cfr. K. DEMMER, Ius Ecclesiae - Ius gratiae. Animadversiones ad relationem inter ius canonicum et ethos christianum, PerRMCL 66 (1977) 5-46.

I prefer to use the term "concretization"[40], since the term "concretization" in contrast "positivation" is suitable for making the different levels visible. The concept of "positivation" in contrast to that seems to remain too much in the abstract. In other words: What has been posited as *ius divinum* is then in need of a concretizing decision whether it is to be recognized as a legal principle or to be transformed into a legal norm. Between divine prescription and legal decision in an individual case several steps of mediation are necessary.

The necessitiy of a concretizing transformation of biblical contents into legal principles and applicable legal norms is unquestionable. Between these two dimensions a basic difference is to be seen. The law is directed towards application and has to meet the needs of the public order and is therefore inevitably influenced by history and a current expression of a certain legal culture with all related implications. The law has a method of its own, specific principles of interpretation and application. Legal norms are based on a lawgiver's decisions, who selects the legally relevant facts and gives them an adequate appearance by an equally selective way of formulating it. This coincides with the intention of "formalization". Norms of Canon Law never represent the divine truth in itself.

From a theoretical point of view, taking into consideration the ontological levels of law, one can conceive the levels of concretization as follows. It emerges as a fourfold step:

(1) Supreme, not further deducible guidelines[41]: values and goods in material regard, basic principles in formal regard whose function is to enable the structure of law as assessing unit. Some of them are based in the Bible.

(2) Partial values, partial goods and system-founding legal principles, which originate from the application of the general legal norms on narrower sectors of reality (for instance the principle of consenting within the marriage law).

(3) The legal system in force with all its legal norms.

(4) The decision in an individual case.

None of these levels is dispensable. A decision in a particular case missing the legal norm would be a juridically unfounded decision. Legal norms,

---

[40] Cfr. to this notion the basic analysis of the term: K. ENGISCH, Die Idee der Konkretisierung in Recht und Rechtswissenschaft unserer Zeit, Heidelberg ²1968.

[41] F. BYDLINSKI, Fundamentale Rechtsgrundsätze. Zur rechtsethischen Verfassung der Sozietät, Wien-New York 1988.

which are not based on values, goods and principles would be without legitimation. No level can simply be derived from the higher ones[42]; getting down from the highest to the lowest, each level shows a greater degree of empirical reality[43].

Some Conclusions and Consequences

The idea of *ius divinum* represents the unassailable aspects and the dimension of the immutable (truth) in Canon Law, although it is in itself not law.

I plead for canonists making use of the hermeneutics within the Old Testament (especially in the relation between the Decalogue and its concretizations and transformations in biblical laws) and within the Bible as a whole.[44] Here lies maybe the first and original hermeneutical key for eliciting and concretizing divine law. Thus canonists would stand to gain new insights into the fundamentals of their work.

The word of God as such is neither moral (ethics) nor law, it underlies these and all other possible aspects (categories). We cannot give the meaning of a law to the word of God. The Bible does not contain the juridical framework of the legal order of the Church, but it does contain the will of God in different formulations, the hermeneutical principles for grasping it and the values and goods necessary for the individual life of the faithful and for the Christian community itself. These values and goods are not yet law. To become law, they have to be transformed into legal principles and applicable law by way of concretization. The rather theological and philosophical concept of promulgation, which is applied to the *ius divinum positivum* (promulgation in the Revelation) as well as to the *ius divinum naturale* (promulgation in the human reason), is not able to meet the requirements of concretization, leaving out the indispensable selective process of defining the single legal norms.

---

[42] E. g. the process of the juridical subsumption is in no way a logical conclusion in regard to the legal norm applied; it rather produces a correspondence between two different categories (the facts and the legal norm) by means of an identical *ratio*, which means the proper sense of the legal norm. Therefore the individual decision contains the reality of the single case, too (cfr. A. KAUFMANN, in: A. KAUFMANN-W. HASSEMER [ed.], Einführung in Rechtsphilosophie und Rechtstheorie der Gegenwart, Heidelberg [6]1994, 162).

[43] With each additional step of concretization the goods, values and principles, which really form the *ius divinum*, are more and more refracted.

[44] Cfr. Vat II, DV 24: *"Sacrae Paginae studium sit veluti anima Sacrae Theologiae."*

The indispensable necessity of the concretization of the will of God - making use of different levels of abstractness - is based in the inner-biblical hermeneutics as well as in the structure of law itself. Each level of concretization must consist of both orientation to the will of God and the facts, to which the law has to be applied.

There is no keen dividing-line between divine law and ecclesiastical law (*ius divinum - ius mere ecclesiasticum*), but there are fluid transitions. It would be necessary to revise the doctrine of the addressee of *ius divinum*.

To take into account the biblical basis of Canon Law turns out to be essential for defining what Canon Law stands for: it has to be law in the proper sense of the word in order to be able to interact with the other legal orders in this world (law of the states, international law, laws of other Christian communities and other religions) and to serve them as a good example, especially in the matter of the inalienable rights of the human being.

The traditional doctrine of immutability and indispensability of the norms of *Ius divinum* must be revised and completely rethought. A certain legal formulation should never be a hindrance in concretizing the will of God, even if a compromise has to be made. The compromise can be closer to God's will than the rigid and severe application of the letter of the law. In any case the solution must be the closest one to the will of God. If these requirements are met, a dispensation of a norm of the *ius divinum* would not be a violation of the will of God, but would rather mean compliance with the spirit of law instead of its letter (cfr. RJ 88 in VI°) - thus carrying out the biblical directive "be merciful, just as your father is merciful" (Lk 6,36). The reason for this lies in the proper concept of the concretization of God's will: Each level of concretization includes a greater degree of reality, for which the legal norm was formulated or the decision in an individual case is made.

An improvement of the doctrine of dispensation could lead to a more differentiated view of the dispensation (especially in regard to decisions for life involving the whole person) distinguishing its character as a mere *declaratory* act on the one hand, and as a *constitutive* act on the other hand. With the declaratory act the authority publicly ascertains that it is no longer possible for the petitioner to adhere to the decision once it has been made. In this case the authority has to rely on the judgement of the individual conscience of the petitioner (cfr. c. 691 § 1 CIC); without taking into consideration this judgement the authority would become guilty due to morally illicit cooperation. The *constitutive* character of the dispensation means that the juridical act overrules the juridical effects of the former decision.[45] This would be rather an expression of tolerance and mercy than an approval of guilt - for the sake of the salvation of man, which is the proper aim of Canon Law.

A comparison between the Catholic and the Protestant practices dealing with Jesus' word on divorce can be stated as follows: the Catholic position stands more or less opposed to the Protestant situation, i.e. the lack of enforceable legal rules in this regard, with the result, "daß der einzelne Pfarrer allein gelassen wird und meist den Weg des geringsten Widerstandes, d.h. der Absegnung alles dessen, was geschehen ist, wählen muß"[46]. Both interpretations lead to great difficulties and insolvable problems: The Catholic Church regards the biblical values and goods too immediately as legal, enforceable rules; the Protestant interpretation undervalues the biblical directives and its normativity, relativizing them. Thus we can conclude: both interpretations disregard the necessity of the concretization of the divine, unassailable guidelines into the human reality. But the biblical hermeneutics itself shows the way for relating the divine and the human to each other in a correct manner.

Prof. Ddr. Mag. Helmuth Pree,
Universität Passau

---

[45] This result, at least in its substance, is shared by K. DEMMER, Ius Ecclesiae (Note 39), and K. DEMMER, Moraltheologie (Note 8), from the point of view of christian ethics, and by R. WEIGAND, Wie unauflöslich ist die Ehe? Kirchenrechtsgeschichtliche Aspekte einer aktuellen Problematik, in: A. FRANTZ (ed.), Glauben Wissen Handeln. Beiträge aus Theologie, Philosophie und Naturwissenschaft zu Grundfragen christlicher Existenz, Festschrift P. KAISER, Würzburg 1994, 161-177, arguing mainly from an historical point of view.
[46] U. LUZ, Evangelium (Note 34) 278.

TEMPORARY REPLACEMENTS OR
NEW FORMS OF MINISTRY:
LAY PERSONS WITH
PASTORAL CARE OF PARISHES

Monsignor Wilhelm Onclin, in whose honor this Chair is named, presented to the canonical world a new possibility regarding pastoral care in parishes when, as *relator* for the *coetus De sacra hierarchia*, he reported in 1976 on the workings of the group. Faced with the growing shortage of priests, the study group was exploring ways in which to provide for pastoral care even when a priest was not available. They proposed that if the shortage were severe, "there may be the need to grant some share in the exercise of pastoral care to some persons not marked with the priestly character, or to some community of persons. In such an instance, however, it is necessary to appoint a priest who moderates this pastoral care."[1]

After several modifications his suggestion eventually bore fruit in the promulgated text of canon 517, §2 of the Code of Canon Law for the Latin Church. Moreover, this provision of the code has not remained a dead letter. Although only an ordained priest can be named pastor of a parish, an increasing number of Catholic communities have been experiencing the phenomenon of deacons and non-ordained persons being appointed to provide for their pastoral care. This development has been welcomed by some as an openness to involving lay persons in official church ministry and a new flexibility in response to pastoral needs; others have been more cautious, concerned that something rich and basic to the Catholic typology of being Church is being lost.

The issue has obvious canonical implications; but it also raises more fundamental questions. Among these is the issue of whether the involvement of lay persons in pastoral care of parishes is something transitory, a temporary measure to fill-in for the shortage of clergy which will be redressed as more men respond to the vocation to priesthood; or is it the

---

[1] *Communicationes*, 8 (1976), 24; trans. John A. RENKEN, "Parishes Without a Resident Pastor: Comments on Canon 517, §2", *CLSA Proceedings*, 50 (1988), 253.

development of new forms of ministry, such that we may be involved in one of those rare but real paradigm shifts in ecclesial life?

Of course we will not be able to answer this question definitively today; only the future will see the ultimate resolution. But in honoring Msgr. Onclin, we can attempt a better understanding of this ecclesial phenomenon, and can explore some of the issues it raises even now, "on the road," as it were, to whatever future the Spirit is leading the Church.

First, let me explain the group on whom these considerations are focused. We are dealing with people who are placed in charge of the pastoral care of a parish or similar ecclesial community. Excluded from the present study are non-ordained persons who work together with a resident pastor, serve on a pastoral team together with a priest, or otherwise do not themselves have the direct responsibility for pastoral care. We are dealing with parishes without a resident pastor, and whose pastoral care depends on a non-ordained person with some supervision or "moderation" by a priest.

These remarks are divided into three parts. As a first step it will be helpful to take a look at the phenomenon itself and how it is being approached in various places around the world. A second step, necessary for a canon lawyer and useful for others in the Church, is to analyze canon 517, §2 and some of the questions which this canon raises today. Finally, we will come to the issue stated above: to what extent are we dealing only with a temporary replacement, a suppletory service, and to what extent is something new emerging in church ministry?

THE PHENOMENON

A. *Some Statistics*[2]

In 1993, the most recent year for which Vatican statistics are available, 3,162 parishes were cared for by permanent deacons, non-ordained religious men and women, and lay persons. This number represents only about 1.5% of the total parishes in the world, but it is also a three-fold

---

[2] See Secretaria Status, Rationarium Generale Ecclesiae, *Statistical Yearbook of the Church*, Vatican City: Typis Polyglottis, n.d.. The most recent edition available to me is for 1993.

increase over the previous fifteen years, for in 1973 there were 1,046 parishes so cared for, or 0.5% of the total parishes that year.

Clearly, we are not talking about a large number of parishes, nor are we dealing with a phenomenon which has reached a stage of major proportions. Yet when examined more closely, we are dealing with facts which impact significant portions of the Church.

For example, while the Church in many nations does not report parishes cared for by non-priests, most of the countries of Western Europe already have some experience with these arrangements, primarily with lay leaders of parishes. France has the greatest reported numbers in Europe, with nearly 3% of French parishes cared for by non-ordained people, primarily lay persons. In Canada, 6% of parishes are in the charge of lay persons. There are lay people in charge of parishes in most of the countries of Latin America.

The situation is more dramatic in certain missionary areas. For example, in Micronesia, 43% of the parishes are cared for by a permanent deacon, and in Namibia deacons care for nearly one-quarter of the parishes. Over half the parishes in French Polynesia are cared for by lay persons, as are a third or more of the parishes in Laos, the Cook Islands, the Asiatic portion of the Russian Federation, and in Guinea Bissau in Africa.

Several factors have given rise to this phenomenon.[3] First, in many countries there is a shortage of clergy, either in absolute terms, or in relationship to the burgeoning Catholic population. For example, in some African countries the ratio of Catholics per priest is quite high: 17,264 in Angola (where 18% of the parishes are cared for by non-priests).[4] Second, in missionary countries the traditional role of the catechist continues to provide for local leadership when clergy are not avail-

---

[3] See Alexander A. VADAKUMTHALA, *Lay Person as Caretaker of a Parish (A Juridical and Theological Study of Canon 517, 2)*, JCD dissertation, Urbaniana University, Rome, 1992, 177-188.

[4] The *Statistical Yearbook of the Church 1993*, 94-101, provides ratios of Catholics per priest. Nearly 10% or more of parishes are staffed by non-ordained persons in Burundi (10,756 Catholics per priest), Sudan (10,635 Catholics per priest), Peru (8,492 Catholics per priest), Gabon (7,303 Catholics per priest), and Zambia (3,964 Catholics per priest).

able to staff parishes or mission stations. For example, catechists are a full-time position, often involving the pastoral care of a parish, in French Polynesia. Finally, under some repressive regimes it has not been possible to recruit adequate clergy, and lay persons are placed in charge of parishes. Such may have been the case, at least in the past, for Laos and the Asiatic portion of the Russian Federation.

It is also important to note in this context that there is a sizeable number of parishes which have no resident pastor, but are cared for by another priest. Worldwide this came to over 55,000 parishes in 1993; that is, more than one out of four existing parishes. As the clergy ages, there will be increasing numbers of such parishes which will either fall vacant, or require a non-priest to provide pastoral care.[5] Taking into account these parishes cared for by a neighboring pastor, those under the care of a non-priest, and those which are totally vacant, over 27% of parishes worldwide lack a resident pastor.

Who is providing the care in parishes without a priest? In the great majority of cases this is still a priest, but one who is not the resident pastor. In those parishes where a non-priest is assigned to provide some form of care, the majority are lay persons (1,614 parishes) or women religious (1,068 parishes). Permanent deacons and non-ordained religious men account for less than 500 parishes.

In some countries the lay persons who have charge of parishes are highly educated, with advanced degrees in theology. In others, a variety of backgrounds can be found although there is increased concern for formal training. In many places, the person who is now given charge of a parish began in some form of catechetics or educational ministry, and gradually expanded into a broader pastoral ministry.[6] The system of

---

[5] The Vatican does not publish statistics on the age of priests worldwide. For a detailed study of the aging of priests in the United States, see Richard A. SCHOENHERR and Lawrence A. YOUNG, *Full Pews and Empty Altars: Demographics of the Priest Shortage in United States Catholic Dioceses,* Madison, WI: University of Wisconsin Press, 1993. The sizeable number of priests reaching retirement age (75 for pastors) far exceeds the number being ordained.

[6] See Ad VAN DER HELM, *Un clergé parallèle?,* Strasbourg: CERDIC, 1993, 75-77, regarding France and The Netherlands. For an in-depth study of several women who are in charge of parishes in the United States, and their backgrounds in coming to this ministry, see Ruth A. WALLACE, *They Call Her Pastor: A New Role for Catholic Women,* Albany, NY: State University of New York Press, 1992.

selection, appointment, supervision, and so on, is not specified in canon law, and varies from country to country, or diocese to diocese.[7]

B. Precedents

The 1983 Code of Canon Law did not invent the practice of lay persons being placed in charge of parishes. Moreover, one need not have recourse to a distant past for precedents.[8] Within recent memory, pastoral necessity and the experience of missionary churches brought about the experience which formed the groundwork for Msgr. Onclin's *coetus*.

A first example may be found in missionary catechists. This is a specialized vocation, usually of a married man, which is structured in various ways depending on the part of the world. In the Pacific Islands, for example, the position of catechist is a full-time, life-long commitment, supported by the Church, and subject to assignment and transfer by the diocesan bishop. In various parts of Latin America, the catechist has been a volunteer, or at most a paid minister for a limited term. In Africa, the role of catechist has gradually evolved in countries such as Zaire, to a recognized category of parish leaders called *bakambi* (plural of *mokambi*).[9]

---

[7] These have been studied in a number of licentiate theses and doctoral dissertations, including: Gerard M. FITZSIMMONS, *Canon 517, §2: Parish Ministry Without Priests?*, JCL thesis, Catholic University of America, Washington, 1987; Kenneth P. LOHRMEYER, *Collaborative Parochial Ministry According to Canon 517, §2*, JCL thesis, Catholic University of America, Washington, 1988; Margaret M. BASTEYNS, *Canon 517, §2 and the Lay Pastoral Administrator: Some Canonical Considerations*, JCL thesis, Catholic University of America, Washington, 1989; Thomas X. HOFMANN, *Alternative Forms of Pastoral Leadership and the Power of Governance: Canon 517, §2 and Developing Practice*, JCL thesis, Catholic University of America, Washington, 1990; Roy M. KLISTER, *Non-Presbyteral Pastoral Care in Parish Liturgical Life: An Historical, Canonical and Theological Study*, DLS dissertation, Anselmianum Athenaeum, Rome, 1991; Alexander A. VADAKUMTHALA, *Lay Person as Caretaker of a Parish (A Juridical and Theological Study of Canon 517, 2)*, JCD dissertation, Urbaniana University, Rome, 1992; Ad VAN DER HELM, *Un clergé parallèle?*, Strasbourg, CERDIC, 1993; Robert L. DELAND, *Some Implications of the Implementation of Canon 517, §2 in the United States*, JCL thesis, Katholieke Universiteit Leuven, Leuven, 1993; Michael BÖHNKE, *Pastoral in Gemeinden ohne Pfarrer: Interpretation von c. 517 §2 CIC/1983*, Münsterischer Kommentar zum Codex Iuris Canonici 12, Essen: Ludgerus Verlag, 1994.

[8] But see the interesting history in Hungary reported by DELAND, *o.c.*, 4.

[9] VADAKUMTHALA, 178. See also Vincent de Paul KWANGA NDJIBU, *Le ministère des Bakambi: implications théologico-juridiques (Can. 517, §2)*, JCD dissertation, Gregorian University, Rome, 1993; Antoine Finifini MATENKADI, "L'expérience pastorale des responsables laïcs de paroisses (*bakambi*) au Zaïre: histoire et perspectives", *Studia Canonica*, 28 (1994), 155-166.

In its decree on the Church's missionary activity, *Ad gentes*, the Second Vatican Council singled out missionary catechists who work full-time and are placed in charge of a community, and asked that they be given their canonical mission in a pubic liturgical ceremony.[10]

Although not technically a "missionary territory", in various Latin American dioceses one solution to the continuing shortage of priests has been to invite women religious to take charge of local communities, particularly in rural areas. It was this experience that led the Secretary of the Code Commission, then Archbishop Castillo Lara, to urge successfully the inclusion of canon 517, §2 at a time in the code revision process when some wished to delete it.[11]

In addition to missionary catechists and the involvement of women religious, after the Second Vatican Council there was a notable increase in the involvement of non-ordained persons in parish ministry along with the priests assigned to a parish.[12] Frequently this was called "team ministry", although in a somewhat broad sense. In Germany and The Netherlands it was given formal recognition;[13] elsewhere, the arrangements tended to be somewhat looser. But the net effect was to introduce an experience of pastoral care by non-priests, such that those involved as well as the parishioners themselves grew more accustomed to it.

The history of the drafting of this canon has been treated at length elsewhere.[14] The only purpose for my addressing its background is to highlight that the canon did not create something new in the Church; it

---

[10] *Ad gentes* 17. This is one of only three mentions of "canonical mission" in Vatican II; the others refer to the canonical mission a bishop receives (*LG* 24) and the one a bishop gives his priests (*PO* 7).

[11] *Communicationes,* 13 (1981), 149.

[12] Although his study took place after the 1983 code, see the extensive involvement documented by Philip J. MURNION et al., *New Parish Ministers: Laity & Religious on Parish Staffs*, New York: National Pastoral Life Center, 1992.

[13] For Germany, see Heribert HEINEMANN, "Die Mitarbeiter des Pfarrers," in *Handbuch des katholischen Kirchenrechts*, ed. Joseph Listl et al., Regensburg, Pustet, 1983, 418-419; for The Netherlands, see VAN DER HELM, *o.c.*, 155-164.

[14] See especially BÖHNKE, *o.c.*, 14-27; HOFMANN, *o.c.*, 13-18; Jean-Marie HUET, "Les nouvelles formes d'office curial (*CIC*, can. 517)", *Nouvelle Revue Théologique,* 113 (1991), 65-66; John A. RENKEN, "Canonical Issues in the Pastoral Care of Parishes Without Priests", *The Jurist,* 47 (1987), 506-510; Heribert SCHMITZ, "'Gemeindeleitung' durch 'Nichtpfarrer-Priester' oder 'Nichtpriester-Pfarrer': Kanonistische Skizze zu dem neuen Modell pfarrlicher Gemeindeleitung des c. 517 §2 CIC", *Archiv für katholisches Kirchenrecht,* 161 (1992), 343-352; VADAKUMTHALA, *o.c.*, 168-176.

took existing experiences and provided a rough framework for them. Just how rough a framework that is will be the topic of the next point, a canonical analysis of the canon and the questions it has raised.

ANALYSIS OF CANON 517, §2

"Ecclesiastical laws are to be understood in accord with the proper meaning of the words considered in their text and context" (c. 17). So let us begin with the text of the canon, place these words in their context, and then explore what all this means.

Canon 517, §2 reads:

> If because of a shortage of priests the diocesan bishop should decide that a participation in the exercise of the pastoral care of a parish is to be given to a deacon or to some other person not marked with the priestly character or to a community of persons, he is to appoint some priest who, endowed with the powers and faculties of a pastor, is to moderate the pastoral care.[15]

The canon is somewhat out of place in its present context. It follows two canons which determine what is a parish and a quasi-parish (cc. 515-516), and precedes the rule on territorial and personal parishes (c. 518). The description of a pastor comes later (c. 519), as well as the prohibition of naming a juridic person as pastor (c. 520). Only several canons later is the rule given that there is to be only one pastor per parish, and one parish per pastor (c. 526). The context, therefore, at least in terms of the placement of the canon in the code, is not very helpful in clarifying its meaning.

The context of paragraph 2 within the canon is obviously set by paragraph 1, which provides for the possibility of a group of priests being named *in solidum* to care for one or several parishes, with one of them serving as "moderator". The moderator is to direct their combined activity and answer for it to the bishop. Later the code clarifies that all the members of the "team" have the duties and functions of a pastor, but are to exercise them in keeping with a mutual arrangement and under the direction of the moderator (c. 543, §1).

---

[15] "Si ob sacerdotum penuriam Episcopus dioecesanus aestimaverit participationem in exercitio curae pastoralis paroeciae concredendam esse diacono aliive personae sacerdotali charactere non insignitae aut personarum communitati, sacerdotem constituat aliquem qui, potestatibus et facultatibus parochi instructus, curam pastoralem moderetur". English translation is my own, in an effort to render the Latin more literally.

Whereas canon 517, §1 looks to all those who are to engage in pastoral care, namely, the priests acting *in solidum* or as a priestly "team", §2 deals only indirectly with those who will carry out the pastoral care. The subject of the paragraph is the bishop naming a priest to moderate the pastoral care carried out by non-priests; only indirectly does it speak about those non-priests and what they do. Again, the context is not very helpful in clarifying the meaning of the law.

So we turn to the issues raised by canon 517, §2. Our analysis will begin with a discussion of the role of the priest in this situation, and then turn to those who actually provide the pastoral care.

A. The Priest who Moderates Pastoral Care

Three issues present themselves here: is he "pastor" of the parish concerned? What are the "powers and faculties of a pastor" with which he is to be endowed, and from whom does he receive them? What does it mean for him to "moderate" the pastoral care of the parish?

1. Is he Pastor?

To resolve this question, it will help to situate this priest in the context of the various ways in which priests provide for the pastoral care of a parish. Leaving aside the positions of parochial vicar (c. 545), chaplain (c. 564), or even rector of a church (c. 556), there are five major ways in which a priest provides pastoral care for a parish. The first is as the resident pastor of a parish. Second, a priest can be named a parochial administrator. Third, he can be a member of a group of priests who *in solidum* provide pastoral care for one or several parishes. Fourth, as pastor of a parish he can be given the pastoral care of neighboring parishes. Fifth, he may be named to moderate the pastoral care provided by deacons or non-ordained persons in a parish. Is the priest a "pastor" in all of these situations?

In the first, he clearly is the pastor. Only a priest can be named as pastor (cc. 150; 521, §1). He cares for the community who are the parish as their proper pastor (c. 515, §1), and therefore cares for them in his own name and not as a vicar or delegate of the bishop. He has extensive responsibilities and rights as determined in the Code of Canon Law (e.g., cc. 528-535), particular law, and custom. He serves for an indefinite term, unless with the agreement of the episcopal conference the bishop has named him for a limited term (c.522). During his time in office he is presumed to have all the authority necessary to carry out his responsibilities, and cannot be transferred against his will or removed from the office except for grave cause (cc. 190, §2; 193, §§1 and 2).

As resident pastor, he may provide pastoral care on his own; or he may be assisted by one or more priests who have been named as parochial vicars (c. 545). He can also be aided by deacons and non-ordained persons (c. 519); if these are given a more formal "share in the exercise of pastoral care" under his direction, we may have one application of canon 517, §2, but this is not the focus of our study of this canon.

A parochial administrator substitutes for an impeded or absent pastor, or cares for a parish which lacks a resident pastor (c. 539). He is not himself a pastor, but he normally enjoys the same rights and duties as a pastor (c. 540, §1). He is limited, however, for he cannot do anything to prejudice the rights of the pastor, and when his function comes to an end he must render an account to the pastor of what he has done (c. 540, §§2 and 3).

The third manner of providing pastoral care, by priests named *in solidum* to provide pastoral care for one or more parishes, was discussed earlier. In this situation the priests acting *in solidum* provide what a pastor would provide, arranging for individual functions among themselves and acting in concord under the direction of their moderator.[16] But is the moderator himself the pastor of the parish? Most commentators are agreed that he is not; there is either no pastor for the parish, or at least it is the group of priests *in solidum* which provides this function.[17] Some,

[16] This arrangement has met with some skepticism by canonists, who are concerned with both the confusion the people may feel ("who's in charge?"), and with possible rivalry among the priests. See Francesco COCCOPALMERIO, "Quaestiones de paroecia in novo Codice", *Periodica*, 73 (1984), 391-393; Heribert HEINEMANN, "Sonderformen der Pfarrgemeindeorganisation gemäss C. 517", *Archiv für katholisches Kirchenrecht,* 163 (1994), 343, and Hans PAARHAMMER, in *Münsterischer Kommentar zum Codex Iuris Canonici*, ed. Klaus Lüdicke, Essen: Ludgerus Verlag, 1985, 517/1, both of whom cite favorably the objections raised during the drafting process by Heribert SCHMITZ, "Pfarrei und Gemeinde", *Archiv für katholisches Kirchenrecht,* 148 (1979), 66. See also Gordon READ, in *The Canon Law: Letter & Spirit*, ed. Gerard Sheehy et al., Collegeville, MN: Liturgical Press, 1995, 286. Patrick VALDRINI, in *Droit canonique*, Paris: Dalloz, 1989, 209, cautions this could easily devolve into a pastor with parochial vicars if particular law does not foster a more "solidaire" approach by the group.

[17] See Juan CALVO, in *Code of Canon Law Annotated*, ed. Ernesto Capparos et al.,

however, see the role of moderator as equivalent to pastor, the other priests being "co-pastors" at a lesser degree of authority.[18]

The fourth manner, by a resident pastor of one parish providing pastoral care for one or more neighboring parishes (c. 526, §1), is an expanded provision in the revised canon law. It reads:

> A pastor is to have parochial care of only one parish; however, due to a shortage of priests or other circumstances, the care of several neighboring parishes can be entrusted to the same pastor.[19]

The priest is clearly the pastor of one parish; is he also the pastor of each of the other parishes where he provides care?[20]

The commentators are divided on this issue. Some view him as clearly the pastor of each of the parishes.[21] They claim the canon pro-

---

Montreal: Wilson & Lafleur, 1993, 380; Jean-Claude PÉRISSET, *La paroisse: Commentaire des Canons 515-572*, Paris: Tardy, 1989, 186; Alain SÉRIAUX, *Droit canonique*, Paris: Presses Universitaires de France, 1996, 290. It is the team itself which is the pastor, even though it is not a juridic person, according to: Francesco COCCOPALMERIO, *De paroecia*, Rome: Pontificia Università Gregoriana, 1991, 192; Marcello MORGANTE, *La parrocchia nel Codice di Diritto Canonico: Commento giuridico-pastorale*, Turin: Edizioni Paoline, 1985, 168; Antonio S. SANCHEZ-GIL, in *Comentario exegético al Código de Derecho Canónico*, vol. 2, Pamplona: EUNSA, 1996, 1215.

[18] Lamberto DE ECHEVERRÍA, in *Código de Derecho Canónico, Edición bilingüe comentada*, ed. Lamberto de Echeverría, 5th ed., Madrid: BAC, 1985, 292-293 emphasizes the role of the moderator, arguing the code is contrary to any egalitarian formula within the priestly group; PAARHAMMER, at c. 517/2, states: "So ist der Moderator eigentlich der *pastor proprius*". Without calling him "curé", HUET, *o.c.*, 63-64, insists on the moderator as the hierarchical authority within the group of priests *in solidum*.

[19] "Parochus unius paroeciae tantum curam paroecialem habeat; ob penuriam tamen sacerdotum aut alia adiuncta, plurium vicinarum paroeciarum cura eidem parocho concredi potest".

[20] This situation is different from the arrangement of parishes with missions traditional in some parts of the world, where the territory of a parish is quite large, and the various towns contained within it are considered "missions" served by the "parish" which is located in the main town; see Richard F. GROVES, "Priestless Parishes: Exploring the Future", *CLSA Proceedings*, 48 (1986), 56-57. Nor is it exactly the same as the pastoral zones or *Pfarrverband* of the German dioceses; see Peter KRÄMER, "Der Pfarrverband", in *Handbuch des katholischen Kirchenrechts*, 429-432.

[21] See: Peter ERDÖ, "De incompatibilitate officiorum, specialiter paroeciarum. Adnotationes ad cann. 152 et 526", *Periodica*, 80 (1991), 499-522; HEINEMANN, "Sonderformen der Pfarrgemeindeorganisation gemäss C. 517", 341; Helmuth PREE, "Priestermangel — Abhilfe durch das neue Kirchenrecht?", *Theologisch-Praktische Quartalschrift*, 132 (1984), 376; VALDRINI, 208. Others point out that even if he need not be named as pastor, this is still possible: Luigi CHIAPPETTA, *Il Codice di Diritto Canonico, Commento giuridico-pastorale*, vol. 1, Naples: Dehoniane, 1988, 624; SANCHEZ-GIL, *o.c.*, 1253-1254

vides an explicit exception to the norm forbidding pastors to have more than one parish. Moreover, the old law's prohibition of holding two different parishes (unless they were equally-principally united[22]) has not been repeated, and its basis (namely, that two offices, each of which required residence, were incompatible) has been weakened since it is permissible for a pastor to reside outside of his parish provided there is a just cause and adequate provision for the performance of parochial functions (c. 533, §1).

Others view this extraordinary situation as authorizing the priest to provide pastoral care, but not as an additional appointment as pastor. Rather, he serves as administrator, or as "pastoral care giver" of the other parishes, which remain parishes without a pastor.[23] This is in effect how they are viewed in the Vatican's *Statistical Yearbook of the Church*. It also means that specific letters of appointment and installation as pastor do not have to be made for each parish, but only for the one for which the priest is pastor; and that if the bishop wishes to change the configuration and the priest is unwilling, he does not have to go through the technical process of removing a pastor to move him out of some of the neighboring parishes.[24]

This question has some bearing on the next option because in these situations of providing care for neighboring parishes, a priest may call on the aid of deacons or non-ordained persons, as another application of canon 517, §2.[25] But again, this is not the application of that canon with which this paper is concerned.

(who says the practice in Spain, however, is to name the pastor as administrator of the other parishes). Georg MAY argues that parishes are no longer incompatible offices: "Das Kirchenamt", in *Handbuch des katholischen Kirchenrechts*, 145. PÉRISSET, *o.c.*, 84-86, in a somewhat confused treatment of this canon, does not say the priest is juridically the pastor of each of the parishes, but says he must take possession of each and concludes the obvious sense of c. 526, §1 is that the priest is *curé* of each of the parishes.

[22] 1917 code c. 460, §1.

[23] See: CALVO, *o.c.*, 386; Norbert RUF, *Das Recht der katholischen Kirche nach dem neuen Codex Iuris Canonici: für die Praxis erläutert*, Freiburg-im-Br.: Herder, 1989, 143.

[24] See discussion of these possibilities in PAARHAMMER, at 526. SANCHEZ-GIL, *o.c.*, 1253-1254 points out that even if the priest is named pastor in several neighboring parishes, this need not be exactly the same in all of them: he could have a term in one but not in another, the appointments could be made at the same or varying times, he could cease from office in one but not others, etc.

[25] See READ, *o.c.*, 291.

Finally, a priest may be involved in pastoral care of a parish indirectly; that is, he serves as the moderator of the pastoral care which is provided directly by a deacon or non-ordained person. Is he pastor in this situation? Some commentators think he is, and point to the fact that he is endowed with the powers and faculties of a pastor.[26] But others point to the complex history of canon 517, §2, where he was listed as the pastor of the parish until the very end of the revision process, when this designation was dropped in order to leave greater flexibility to local situations.[27]

Given the complex possibilities we have just explored, there are many ways in which the priest could be related to the parish. However, since a shortage of priests is given as the reason for this special arrangement, it appears most likely that the parish is to be considered to be without a resident pastor, and that the priest's role is not as pastor of the parish but as moderator of those who provide pastoral care.[28]

2. His Function

The moderator is "endowed with the powers and faculties of a pastor". Canon 519 describes the pastor as "the proper shepherd of the parish", "exercising pastoral care", and carrying out the "duties of teaching, sanctifying and governing". These are his powers, which are more fully described in their various aspects by canons in Books II, III, IV, and V of the code. In addition, the law extends to pastors a variety of faculties.[29] It also specifies a variety of duties which are specific to his office.[30]

---

[26] PÉRISSET, o.c., 204-205; this is also the practical determination in some U.S. dioceses according to RENKEN, "Canonical Issues in the Pastoral Care of Parishes Without Priests", 512. See also the mistaken approach of the Austrian bishops as reported in SCHMITZ, "'Gemeindeleitung' durch 'Nichtpfarrer-Priester' oder 'Nichtpriester-Pfarrer'", 356, note 94.

[27] The specification of the moderator as a pastor was omitted "per non ridurre eccessivamente la portata di questa nuova figura né cortare troppo l'ambito di competenza di questi incaricati". Communicationes, 13 (1981), 149.

[28] This seems to be the consensus of the commentators. Even VALDRINI, o.c., 211, who says the office of pastor is not vacant, admits the priest moderator is not a pastor in the code's sense.

[29] For example: to confirm when he receives baptized adults into full communion (c. 883, 2°) and in danger of death (c. 883, 3°); to administer the sacrament of penance (c. 968, §1); to delegate deacons and priests to do assist at marriages in the parish (c. 1111, §1); to dispense from private vows (c. 1196, 1°), promissory oaths (c. 1203), the obligations of feast days or days of penance (c. 1245), and from most occult marriage impediments of ecclesiastical law in situations of danger of death or omnia parata (cc. 1079, §2 and 1080).

[30] E.g., residence, Missa pro populo, etc. — cc. 533, §1 and 544. Many of his rights

Not all of these pertain to the moderator in a canon 517, §2 situation. He is not a pastor in his own right, and so does not have all the obligations that come with the office of pastor. Moreover, the wording of the canon was deliberately left in general terms to provide flexibility for local bishops to work out the specifics of these situations. Hofmann reviews four opinions concerning the situation of the moderator, and concludes the one which most respects the freedom of the local bishop is that the moderator has all the powers and faculties of a pastor (but not the duties), but unlike a resident pastor, he does not have these to the exclusion of others.[31] Thus the diocesan bishop can specify other persons as exercising some of these powers without infringing on the juridic figure of the moderator.

This raises a further question: does this canon grant these powers and faculties by law, or does it describe the powers and faculties the diocesan bishop is to give the priest? The canon itself is not explicit on this, for it could be read as describing what the bishop does in naming the priest or as detailing what the juridic figure of the position entails. However, it does seem that the moderator has an office — a function constituted by law in a stable manner to be exercised for a spiritual purpose (c. 145, §1). The law is supposed to provide for the obligations and rights that go with an office (c. 145, §2), so it would seem that the "powers and faculties of a pastor" are included by law with the office of moderator, although the diocesan bishop can adjust the exercise of these since the moderator does not have exclusive claim to them, such as a pastor might have.

Central to his function is to "moderate" the pastoral care being given by the non-ordained in the parish, but the code does not give much clarification on what this means. Huet, after examining a number of uses of "moderate" in the code, proposes that the moderator of the curia be used as to understand by analogy the priest moderator in a canon 517, §2 situation: both work directly under the bishop, and their principal concern is to coordinate the activity of those who work for the curia or the parish.[32] Coccopalmerio suggests two major functions arise from the word "moderate": to exercise vigilance over those who are participating

are also obligations. For a more detailed discussion of pastors, see Francesco Cocco-Palmerio, "De parochis", *Periodica,* 78 (1989), 55-112.

[31] Hofmann, *o.c.*, 29-32.

[32] Huet, *o.c.*, 62.

in pastoral care, and to provide for the exercise of priestly orders when needed.[33] This does not exclude, of course, the possibility of another priest providing the sacramental services.[34] Indeed, the moderator may wind up dealing with the parish primarily through writing or telephone contact, rather than providing direct service in the parish.[35] In effect, this seems to be an area where greater precision could be given by particular law, or at least in the appointment of the priest to this office (c. 145, §2).

Finally, his position does not enjoy the stability associated with the office of pastor, and he is movable *ad nutum episcopi.*[36] He has no set term of office unless that is provided in particular law, nor does the general law set an age limit on serving as priest moderator.

B. Lay Persons Participating in Pastoral Care

The canon mentions "a deacon or... some other person not marked with the priestly character or... a community of persons". A deacon is an ordained cleric; he shares in the sacrament of holy orders, and is incardinated in virtue of diaconal ordination. He enjoys the obligations and rights proper to clergy. His status in law is different from persons who are not ordained. While he is "not marked with the priestly character", the deacon is nonetheless a special case and for the purposes of today's study, will be left to one side so that we might concentrate on the majority of non-priests participating in pastoral care, those who in law are termed laity.

The distinction between clergy and laity is based on the sacrament of orders; lay persons are those who have not been ordained (c. 207, §1). This includes women religious, men religious who are not ordained, and all others commonly called "lay persons". Because of their common condition of being non-ordained, this is the group of persons who are classified as "lay persons" participating in pastoral care.

---

[33] COCCOPALMERIO, *De paroecia*, 110.

[34] This second priest is presumed as normal in Barbara Anne CUSACK and Therese Guerin SULLIVAN, *Pastoral Care in Parishes Without a Pastor: Applications of Canon 517, §2*, Washington, DC: Canon Law Society of America, 1995, 31-34.

[35] SCHMITZ, "'Gemeindeleitung' durch 'Nichtpfarrer-Priester' oder 'Nichtpriester-Pfarrer'", 359 refers to the possibility of "Schreibtischpriester" or "Telefonpriester" — might one also speak of the "e-mail priest" these days?

[36] Ibid.

The canon also provides for a "community" to participate in pastoral care. This could be a recognized canonical entity, such as a religious or secular institute, a society of apostolic life without vows, a recognized association of the faithful, and so on; or, it could be an *ad hoc* group who come together for this specific purpose, and who as a unit (rather than as individuals) are willing to be named to this service.

1. The Parish

Central to this canon is the parish. Canon 517, together with the related canons discussed earlier about pastors, are all focused on how pastoral care will be provided to a parish. What is a parish?

Under the previous code, the parish was a benefice;[37] basically, a benefice was how the priest was paid. The Second Vatican Council separated the issue of income from that of pastoral care, and focused on the spiritual dimension of pastoral ministry;[38] but the focus remained on the priest: where the priest provided care. Current church law has shifted the focus to the community of persons who make up the parish. They are a communion of the faithful, within the broader portion of God's people who constitute the diocese, established by the bishop in such a way that pastoral care can be provided to them in an effective manner.

Normally this community is identified by means of territory. But it can also be determined according to some other criteria: rite, language, nationality (c. 518), university community (c. 813), etc. In the United States it is not unknown to have several parishes overlap the same territory, one a "territorial" parish, another based on language or ethnic background, and a third centered around a local university. Each of these parishes is a way of organizing pastoral care; each is also a center of mission.

The parish is a juridic person in law; it has its own right to exist, the right to a variety of spiritual and material services, the right to be protected and safeguarded by higher church authority such as the diocesan bishop. It has a fundamental right to pastoral care.[39]

---

[37] 1917 code c. 1409: "Beneficium ecclesiasticum est ens iuridicum a competente ecclesiastica auctoritate in perpetuum constitutum seu erectum, constans officio sacro et iure percipiendi reditus ex dote officio adnexos".

[38] *Presbyterorum Ordinis* 20.

[39] See James A. CORIDEN, "The Foundations of the Rights of Parishes: The Bases for

The usual church official responsible for seeing to the pastoral care, and safeguarding the rights of a parish is the pastor. As discussed earlier, a variety of other arrangements can be made to assure this pastoral care, but none of them affect the existence of the parish as such. The parish remains, even as different modes for assuring its pastoral care may come and go.

2. Pastoral Care

The dimensions of pastoral care are quite broad. As an expression of Church, the parish is a communion of the faithful. This communion is ultimately with God, who is a communion of three divine persons. But it is also a communion of parishioners with one another. Both dimensions are expressed and nourished in the Holy Communion of the Eucharist, and bonded with the rest of the Catholic communion through the hierarchical communion of those who preside at the Eucharist. A first component of pastoral care, therefore, is to foster this communion, to nourish it through the Eucharist, and to develop those bonds among people that make it possible for someone to experience being "at home" in the parish.

Likewise, as a realization of Church the parish is mission. Mission has its source in God, whose inner life we understand in terms of the divine missions. Christ came to us on mission, and sent the Spirit to continue his mission throughout time in the Church. The faithful bonded in communion continue Christ's mission in their time and place. Christ's mission is commonly summed up in the messianic triad of prophet, priest and king; pastoral care continues his mission through the functions of teaching, sanctifying, and governing on behalf of the community, even as the members of the community in their own way continue this mission in the world (c. 204).

This theological foundation for pastoral care finds organizational expression in the various canons detailing the teaching, sanctifying, and governing responsibilities of the pastor, discussed earlier. Lay persons

the Canonical Rights of Parishes and Other Local Catholic Communities", in *Ius in Vita et in Missione Ecclesiae*, ed. Pontifical Council for the Interpretation of Legal Texts, Vatican City: Libreria Editrice Vaticana, 1994, 505-525; idem, "The Rights of Parishes: The Canonical Rights and Obligations of Roman Catholic Parishes and Other Local Congregations of the Catholic Faithful", *Studia Canonica*, 28 (1994), 293-309; idem, "The Vindication of Parish Rights", *The Jurist*, 54 (1994), 22-39; James H. PROVOST, "The Rights of the Local Church", *Church*, 5 (1989), 5-9.

who participate in pastoral care, participate in varying degrees in the building up of the communion, and in carrying out the functions of teaching, sanctifying, and governing.

3. Participation in Pastoral Care

There are different degrees of pastoral care. The "full" care of souls requires the exercise of priestly orders, and so is reserved to an ordained priest (c. 150). Any other exercise of pastoral care is partial, and is termed a "participation" in pastoral care. Some lay people cooperate in the care a pastor provides (c. 519), but this is less than the participation of those assigned in virtue of canon 517, §2. Similarly, all the baptized participate in the Church's mission (c. 216), but the participation in virtue of canon 517, §2 is more specific to a parish community, and of a more official character in the communion of the Church.

The degree to which lay people participate in a parish's care in virtue of canon 517, §2 is not specified in the canon itself; that has been left for local determination. Who makes this determination? When a priest is assigned to be a parochial vicar, his participation in the pastor's pastoral care for the parish is determined primarily by his letter of appointment from the bishop and in the mandate given him by the pastor (c. 548, §1). Does something similar apply to the lay persons who participate in pastoral care?

Canon 517, §2 is so silent on details, that this parallel place may provide a way to resolving situations where there is no particular law or custom (c. 19). Particular law, however, could specify not only the lay persons' functions in these cases, but also the church official responsible for making further specifications.[40]

What is clear is that the lay person cannot participate in those aspects of pastoral care which require the exercise of sacred orders; so, the lay person may not celebrate the Eucharist for the parish, confirm, celebrate the sacrament of reconciliation, or anoint the sick. The lay person may

---

[40] Several commentators discuss in detail the kinds of activities the lay person could be assigned in pastoral care. See, for example, BÖHNKE, o.c., 55-69; KLISTER, o.c., 170-223; RENKEN, "Canonical Issues in the Pastoral Care of Parishes Without Priests", 519; idem, "Parishes Without a Resident Pastor: Comments on Canon 517, §2", 257; SANCHEZ-GIL, o.c., 1218.

not preach a homily, which is restricted to someone in sacred orders,[41] although the lay person may preach in the church (c. 766).

This participation in pastoral care is subject to the priest moderator. The French bishops and some commentators see the lay persons and the priest moderator as forming a unit, an *équipe d'animation pastorale*.[42] Others recognize the possibility of greater distance, so that the priest moderator would not be in such regular contact as, for example, some other priest who is the "sacramental priest" for the parish.[43] The parish may or may not experience Sunday celebrations without a priest.

Particular law could specify more accurately the relationship of the priest moderator and the lay person in terms of parish structures. Who attends meetings of the parish pastoral council, the parish finance council, and other parish organizations? Who maintains the parish books, both financial and sacramental? Who acts as "agent" for the parish? Although the presumption of several commentators is that this goes with the position of priest moderator,[44] by particular law the bishop could determine otherwise (c. 1279, §1).

4. Ecclesiastical Office

Is the position of a lay person who participates in the pastoral care of a parish an ecclesiastical office?[45] We saw earlier that the priest moderator's position is considered an ecclesiastical office, although not the office of pastor. For the position of the lay person to be considered an ecclesiastical office, it must meet the criteria set in canon 145: a function for a spiritual purpose, constituted by divine or ecclesiastical office, in a stable manner.

---

[41] Canon 767, §1; see also the Commission for the Authentic Interpretation of the Code, response of May 26, 1987: *AAS,* 79 (1987), 1249.

[42] Les Évêques de France, Bureau d'Études Doctrinales, *Les ministres ordonnés dans une Église-communion*, Paris: Cerf, 1993, 55; see Alphonse BORRAS, "La notion de curé dans le Code de Droit Canonique", *Revue de Droit Canonique,* 37 (1987), 235; Joseph A. JANICKI, in *The Code of Canon Law: A Text and Commentary*, ed. James A. Coriden et al., New York/Mahwah, NJ: Paulist, 1985, 418; SANCHEZ-GIL, *o.c.*, 1218.

[43] See CUSACK and SULLIVAN; SCHMITZ, "'Gemeindeleitung' durch 'Nichtpfarrer-Priester' oder 'Nichtpriester-Pfarrer'", 359.

[44] See, for example, RENKEN, "Parishes Without a Resident Pastor: Comments on Canon 517, §2", 256-257.

[45] Not all commentators address the issue of whether this is an ecclesiastical office. However, that it is an office is affirmed by MORGANTE, *o.c.*, 197, and PÉRISSET, *o.c.* 202.

The function is clearly for a spiritual purpose. It is capable of being erected into an ecclesiastical office, and can be held by a lay person (c. 228, §1). But the wording of canon 517, §2 is so indirect in terms of the lay person that it is difficult to say that the other qualifications are met. Ultimately, this is another matter which seems to be left to particular law.

The code provides two ways in which an ecclesiastical office can be constituted. One is by a law (c. 145, §1). For example, a diocesan law could create the office of a lay person who participates in pastoral care, determine the obligations and rights that go with the office, and resolve various other issues in terms of how the lay person relates to the parish structures, the priest moderator, and the diocese. A second way to constitute an office is by the individual decree which both creates the office and names a person to the office (c. 145, §2). Because we are addressing more than a temporary delegation to perform some function, but rather an on-going relationship of pastoral care, it is likely that even a letter of appointment without other particular law to specify the position as an office, would result in the post being an ecclesiastical office.

Why is this a question worth addressing? There are certain legal effects which follow if the position is an ecclesiastical office. The position itself has to be established by a competent authority; it cannot be assumed by personal initiative, or be instituted by parishioners on their own. Once established, it has the stability inherent in the notion of an ecclesiastical office; it should have a certain duration, and not be started and stopped at whim.

The office is entitled to a description of its rights and obligations (c. 145, §2). This can be done either through particular law or by decree of the bishop in appointing a person to this position. The same authorities can specify further the qualifications for the office, and the extent to which the office holder will enjoy stability (e.g., through appointment for a term). Transfer or removal is protected to some extent by the provision of the canons (cc. 190-195).

Who appoints the lay person to this office? The code presumes the diocesan bishop appoints by free conferral to any of the offices in his diocese, unless this is otherwise specified. The bishop, therefore, not only appoints the priest who moderates their work, but also the lay persons who participate in the pastoral work. Moreover, experience shows that the involvement of the bishop is an important factor in the success of the lay person's service.[46]

5. Title

Finally, there is the question of what to call the lay person who participates in pastoral care in virtue of canon 517, §2. Again the canon leaves this up to local determination. Certain titles would appear to be inappropriate because they could cause confusion as to the non-ordained status of the person providing pastoral care; so, lay pastor, parochial vicar, parish administrator, chaplain, or rector would be inappropriate.[47]

However, in Italy the term "suora parroco" is common, although it has the inconvenience of being limited to women religious and uses the term "pastor" in the title.[48] Ruth Wallace has found that "they call her pastor" is indeed a developing practice among the faithful in the United States.[49] This is an example of how local custom will develop a terminology independent of whatever theological or canonical considerations we might make, and custom is, after all, the best interpreter of law (c. 27).

TEMPORARY REPLACEMENTS OR NEW FORMS OF MINISTRY

To what extent are we assisting at a passing phenomenon, and to what extent is a new form of ministry developing in the Church? Views on this are varied.

First, there is no way at this stage of the development to predict factually whether the phenomenon is passing, or becoming incorporated into the Catholic typology of Church. What follows must therefore be more a question of theory; i.e., should it be allowed or even encouraged to develop, or must it be clearly restricted to a temporary measure?

---

[46] Les Évêques de France, 53-54; see also Wallace's study of individual cases.

[47] See cc. 521, §1 ("pastor" must be a priest), 546 ("parochial vicar" must be a priest), 539 ("parochial administrator" is a priest), 564 ("chaplain" is a priest), and 556 ("rectors of churches" are priests).

[48] See Massimo BOAROTTO, La Parrocchia fra Pastoral e Diritto in Italia: Sua identità e cammino alla luce delle norme canoniche e concordatarie, Rome: Pontificia Univesitas Urbaniana, 1991, 108; MORGANTE, 193-198.

[49] Ruth A. WALLACE, They Call Her Pastor: A New Role for Catholic Women.

A. How Temporary a Measure

Canon 517, §2 begins with: "If because of a shortage of priests" (*Si ob sacerdotum penuriam*).[50] This is one of three canons which mention this condition, the other two dealing with the parochial care of several neighboring parishes by the pastor of one of them (c. 526, §1), and the situation when a local ordinary may permit bination or trination by priests in the diocese (c. 905, §2).

This is more than a temporary absence of clergy, which is addressed in different terms, either by "where there are no priests" (*ubi desunt sacerdotes*),[51] or by "when ministers are lacking" (*deficientibus ministris*),[52] or "when the ordinary minister is absent or impeded" (*absente aut impedito ministro ordinario*).[53] An authentic interpretation of canon 230, §3 makes it clear that the physical absence or unavailability of clergy is what is meant by this temporary absence, at least in terms of when lay persons may distribute the Eucharist.[54]

But in canon 517, §2 we are not dealing with a temporary absence; rather, as with the other two canons where the phrase is used, a more long-term situation is envisioned. This reflects the conciliar use of the phrase, where it regularly meant a situation of shortage requiring others to send help. Those who would help needed to be adequately prepared, and the presumption was that they would have to stay for some time because of the gravity of the situation.[55] From this perspective the phrase used in canon

---

[50] CHIAPPETTA, 616, observes this is the sole canonical cause for what follows.

[51] Canon 541, §1 on what to do when a parish is impeded or vacant and there are no other priests in the parish; and c. 1112, §1 on an authorized lay person assisting at marriage.

[52] Canon 230, §3, as a condition for lay persons to perform certain ministries such as the ministry of the word, presiding over liturgical prayers, conferring baptism, or distributing the Eucharist, etc.; and c. 1248, §2, dealing with what to do if there is no priest to celebrate Mass on Sunday.

[53] Canon 861, §2, on baptism by catechist or other person deputed by the local ordinary.

[54] Commission for the Authentic Interpretation of the Code, February 20, 1987: *AAS*, 80 (1988), 1373: "Utrum minister extraordinarius sacrae communionis, ad normam cann. 910, §2 et 230, §3 deputatus, suum munus suppletorium exercere possit etiam cum praesentes sint in ecclesia, etsi ad celebrationem eucharisticam non participantes, ministri ordinarii, qui non sint quoquo modo impediti? *Responsum*: Negative".

[55] See *Christus Dominus* 6 (bishops to prepare clergy and auxiliaries to send to other churches suffering from a shortage of clergy); *CD* 35 (religious can be asked to help if the diocese where they are located suffers a shortage of diocesan clergy); *Ad gentes* 19

517, §2, while indicating an emergency situation, has the connotation that this is a long-term situation, not a temporary or momentary problem.

Some who have commented on the canon argue that it is tied to very precise circumstances which are transitory, and that the situation must be abandoned when the circumstances change.[56] According to Klister, an artificial shortage must not be created, and other remedies should be tried first, such as combining parishes, reducing the number of priests in teaching posts, etc.[57] It could also be argued that the bishop should first consider other means of providing for a parish — for example, increasing the number of parishes cared for by existing pastors or teams of priests *in solidum* — as well as increase the number of available clergy by denying early retirement, extending retirement age beyond 75, and so forth. Some of these ideas have the ring of desperation about them, and fail to recognize the complex pastoral realities involved.

Coccopalmerio is perhaps more to the point when he comments that the decision about a shortage really has to be made by the local bishop, the official on the spot who has a sense of the pastoral situation. He considers the canonical norm wide enough to permit the bishop to retain a sufficient priest staff for the seminary and for diocesan offices, even while declaring a shortage of clergy for parish assignments.[58] Others confirm that the main point is not the material shortage of clergy, but the pastoral decision of the bishop about the placement of the clergy available to the diocese.[59]

Complicating the situation is the fact that particular law is developing to regulate canon 517, §2 situations, and indeed is being called for by most canonists who have studied the situation. Some of the particular law is faulty,[60] but this does not invalidate the need for legislation which

---

(other churches to help missionary ones suffering from a shortage); *AG* 20 (even if they suffer a shortage, missionary churches to send some of their clergy as missionaries elsewhere); *AG* 38 (bishops to send some of their best priests to missionary dioceses suffering from a shortage of clergy); *Presbyterorum Ordinis* 10 (priests are to be ready to go and serve in dioceses suffering from a shortage of clergy).

[56] VALDRINI, *o.c.*, 210.

[57] KLISTER, 216-217. See also RENKEN, "Parishes Without a Resident Pastor: Comments on Canon 517, §2", 256.

[58] COCCOPALMERIO, *De paroecia*, 108.

[59] BÖHNKE, *o.c.*, 35-37; BORRAS, *o.c.*, 232-233.

[60] See the critiques by BÖHNKE, *o.c.*, 72-88; DELAND, *o.c.*, 28-76; RENKEN, "Canonical Issues in the Pastoral Care of Parishes Without Priests", 510-515; SCHMITZ, "'Gemeindeleitung' durch 'Nichtpfarrer-Priester' oder 'Nichtpriester-Pfarrer'", 354-358.

will provide order, structure, and clear lines of responsibility. Yet the development of this body of law gives the impression that a new form of ministry is developing, rather than a temporary replacement.

Moreover, over a period of time a cadre of competent lay persons is developing who are capable of providing reliable pastoral care in parishes. As the standards of formation are strengthened, as dioceses become increasingly aware of the need for quality control and not just good will, and as people dedicate more of their lives to this service, an expectation is arising that this new class of ministers in the Church will be afforded the kind of remuneration, benefits, and job security appropriate to their service.[61]

Their appointment is more than a temporary deputation, even though the condition for their office is the shortage of priests. It seems closer to the council's provision that bishops could entrust lay persons with certain functions closely connected with the bishop's own pastoral office, including the care of souls — a provision which was not conditioned by the shortage of priests.[62] But would it be in keeping with the meaning of *ob sacerdotum penuriam* to remove them solely because an ordained priest suddenly becomes available? Yet can a parish be denied the services of a resident pastor just because a lay person has been providing various forms of pastoral care for several years?

The difficulty seems to be that the solution is designed as a "stop-gap" measure. In the large scale there is not much indication that the situation for which it is designed is going to cease very soon, even if in individual cases a priest becomes available. Yet as one commentator has remarked, if lay persons remain in pastoral care for a prolonged period of time, there could be "not only an impoverishment of the sacramental life of the parish, but also a certain clericalization of the lay persons".[63] The new form of ministry which may become acceptable could easily be a major shift in the Catholic typology of Church, but could happen merely by default.

---

[61] See DeLand, *o.c.*, 98-103; Van der Helm, *o.c.*, 227-229.

[62] *Apostolicam actuositatem* 24: "Denique hierarchia laicis munia quaedam committit, quae propius cum officiis pastorum coniuncta sunt, ut in propositione doctrinae christianae, in quibusdam actibus liturgicis, in cura animarum".

[63] Sanchez-Gil, *o.c.*, 1219; see also Vadakumthala, *o.c.*, 248-255.

B. Summing Up

In answer to the question posed at the start of this paper, let me offer the following summary points.

The revised code has opened up a number of alternative ways to provide for pastoral care of parishes. This reflects a shift in focus in the code from concentrating on the clergy, to putting the Christian faithful as primary.[64] Canon 517, §2 is one of these alternatives, designed for the situation when there is a shortage of priests.

There are indications that the canon 517, §2 situation is more than a temporary replacement.

1. Canon 517, §2 is not a momentary replacement of missing ministers (such as those canons which specify "when ministers are lacking", etc.). It even presumes a priest is at least available to be appointed moderator.
2. Implementing canon 517, §2 entails the establishment of ecclesiastical offices — at least the office of the priest moderator, and most likely also the ecclesiastical office of the lay person who participates in pastoral care.
3. Particular law is developing — and is desired — to regulate in greater detail and for the long term the canon 517, §2 situation. This gives further evidence that we are dealing with more than a temporary replacement.

But is it also a new form of ministry? Here are some considerations:

1. A cadre of experienced lay persons is developing who have provided pastoral care, and are available for continuing to do so in the same or different parishes. There is reason to consider them a developing profession within the Church.
2. Even as they regret the loss of a resident pastor, there is a receptivity on the part of parishioners to this ministry by lay persons.
3. Lay persons who provide pastoral care are protected by particular law, and in some cases even by civil law. They are developing a

[64] See Eugenio CORECCO, "Theological Justifications of the Codification of the Latin Canon Law", in The New Code of Canon Law. Fifth International Congress of Canon Law, Ottawa, 1984, ed. Michel Thériault and Jean Thorn, Ottawa: Faculty of Canon Law, Saint Paul University, 1986, 84-94.

kind of legal status in the Church, even as they remain lay persons canonically.

4. It appears likely that the general condition of the shortage of priests will get worse before it gets better, which means that the canon 517, §2 situations will continue, and probably will continue to increase in number. Therefore, the pastoral care of parishes by lay persons may well become a *de facto* feature of Catholic parish life for some years to come.

Before concluding, however, that this does constitute a new stable form of ministry, parallel with that provided by ordained clergy, some underlying issues need to be addressed which go beyond statistical observations and the provisions of canon law.

C. Some Underlying Issues

Designed as a temporary solution, canon 517, §2 is nonetheless pointing up some very serious underlying issues. We can only sketch briefly some of these. The first relates to the nature of the local Church, the second addresses the understanding of the priesthood, and a third is related to church renewal as we prepare for a new millennium.

1. Nature of the Local Church

Central to the Catholic tradition of local church is that the one who presides in the community, presides at its worship; and that the summit and source of Christian life is the celebration of the Eucharist. A basic flaw in the canon 517, §2 situation is that the one who effectively leads the community on a day-to-day basis, is not empowered (because not ordained a priest) to lead the community in its eucharistic worship.

The severing of this bond is significant. Joseph Komonchak has identified three results: the effective sundering of pastoral ministry, which Vatican II had attempted to reintegrate; the disruption of the relationship between the Church and the Eucharist; "the third is to bring into danger a proper appreciation of the need for a sacrament of ordination".[65] Admittedly the law provides for a variety of alternatives for otherwise vacant parishes, but all of them depend on an adequate supply of ordained priests; this supply is not always available, nor does the future promise much relief. As noted earlier, already 27% of parishes world-

---

[65] Joseph A. KOMONCHAK, "Church and Ministry", *The Jurist,* 43 (1983), 286-287.

wide lack a resident pastor: what does this say about the nature of the parish as a eucharistic community?

2. Understanding of the Priesthood

The priesthood of the baptized and the ministerial priesthood of the ordained both participate in the priesthood of Christ. They are closely interrelated, but nonetheless they differ "in essence and not simply in degree".[66] But what is this essential difference? The council saw it in terms of the functions the ministerial priest performs: he forms and governs the priestly people, and offers the Eucharist in the name of the people.[67] But if the forming and governing functions are carried out in practice by non-ordained persons, what does this say about the practical understanding of the priesthood? Does it reduce the priest to someone who merely confects sacraments?

This carries with it the danger of emptying the meaning of the sacramentality of holy orders, a sign within the community, instituted by Christ to give grace. Yet given the lack of consensus on the meaning of the priesthood in the Church, it is not surprising that such a trend could take place.[68]

One solution might be to adjust the requirements for ordination, admitting into holy orders those who are being assigned by bishops to participate in the pastoral care of parishes, but continuing to keep them under the supervision of a priest moderator until such time as they are able to minister on their own.[69] This could eventually provide for ordained pastors increasing numbers of parishes, but the difficulty, of course, is that this would also require a change in the Latin Church's discipline on celibacy in regard to married men, and would run counter to the doctrinal position that the Catholic Church is not authorized to ordain women to the priesthood.[70]

---

[66] *Lumen gentium* 10: "Sacerdotium autem fidelium et sacerdotium ministeriale seu hierarchicum, licet essentia et non gradu tantum differant, ad invicem tamen ordinantur".

[67] Ibid.

[68] See the analysis of seven or more major approaches in contemporary theology to understanding the priesthood, in Daniel DONOVAN, *What are they saying about the ministerial priesthood?*, Mahwah, NJ: Paulist, 1992.

[69] This would be an adaptation of the "apprenticeship" approach to priestly formation in c. 235, §2.

[70] Ordination of married men is already taking place in the Latin Church, but on a limited scale. See "Canonical Implications Related to the Ordination of Married Men to the Priesthood in the United States", report of an ad hoc committee to the Canon Law Soci-

But even in the practical sphere, would such a solution work? There are indications that many lay persons who are engaged in the pastoral care of parishes desire a less controlled situation in which to serve, and do not desire priestly ordination.[71] There is insufficient data to determine how wide-spread such a view may be, but it urges caution to those who might see ordination as the solution. Moreover, other main line churches which do admit married clergy, and even ordain women, are experiencing a drastic decrease in the numbers of candidates for ordination. The shortage is not just a "Catholic" phenomenon.

Another solution, long advocated by higher church officials, is a better distribution of clergy. Pius XII urged European bishops to release their priests to serve in Africa,[72] John XXIII did the same for European and North American bishops in regard to Latin America,[73] and the Congregation for the Clergy regularly encourages a better distribution of clergy. The code provides a preference for a priest who would be willing to serve where there is a shortage, provided his own diocese does not suffer from a true necessity (c. 270, §1).

This has worked in the past. The number of European priests who passed through Leuven in preparation for ministry in North and South America bears testimony to this approach. But the decline in the numbers of candidates for the priesthood, at least relative to the needs of all the local churches, makes this solution more difficult to implement.

Is there perhaps another aspect of ecclesial reality which also needs to be addressed if a solution to vacant parishes is to be found? For this, we turn to some concluding reflections on church renewal as we prepare for the third millennium.

3. Church Renewal

If law can be understood only in context, the same is true of the pastoral situation we have been addressing. It can be understood only in the context of church renewal, a process which in many ways has only begun. Major councils have often taken several hundred years to work

ety of America, June 1, 1996. For the doctrinal position on the ordination of women, see John Paul II, apostolic letter *Ordinatio sacerdotalis*, May 22, 1994.

[71] VAN DER HELM, *o.c.*, 209-213.

[72] Pius XII, encyclical letter *Fidei donum* April 21, 1957: *AAS*, 49 (1957), 225-248.

[73] See various letters by John XXIII in Pontificia Commissione per l'America Latina, *Notiziario*, 2 (June 1963).

their way into the pattern or typology of Catholic life. The process was often painful, never simplistic, and frequently marked with what seemed to the people at the time as reversals in direction.[74]

It could be that we are indeed faced with only a temporary situation, that as the renewal of the Church begins to take root not only in structures but in patterns of decision-making, interpersonal relations, and community expectations, a changed manner of ministering by ordained persons will lead to increased candidates and more adequate numbers of priests to pastor local parishes. But it could also be that the Spirit is working something extraordinary in our midst, that the Catholic typology based on the local celebration of the Eucharist is undergoing some form of shift, and that what our parishes will look like in the future we can hardly begin to imagine at this stage in the process.

What can be done in the interim? First, there is the example from the Civil Rights Movement in the United States, and similar efforts on behalf of human dignity elsewhere. Their basic position has been to hold the establishment to the ideals it proclaims. In the Church, this means to hold ourselves and all others in the Church to the standards for ecclesial life set forth by the Second Vatican Council.

Second, as Catholics there is a specific sacramental way of being Church for which we are accountable. Particularly at the parish level, have the layers of bureaus, commissions, plans, and programs which we have developed in recent years obscured the fundamental reality of who we are as a communion in mission?

Finally, whatever the Spirit works in our midst will involve people. We collaborate with the Spirit when we show continued respect for the dignity of all those who work in and for the Church, when we pay attention to the formation of future generations of committed Christians, and when we as a Church take seriously that the salvation of souls is, after all, the supreme law.

Prof. Dr. James H. Provost,
The Catholic University of America,
Washington D.C.

---

[74] See the various studies of the colloquium, *La Reception y la Comunión entre las Iglesias*, Salamanca, April 8-14, 1996, which will be published shortly in various languages.

Personalia

HELMUTH PREE was born in 1950 in Reichental (Austria). He studied law (dr. iur., Linz, 1974), Canon Law (J.C.D., Pontifical Lateran University, Rome, 1981) and Theology (Magister, Linz, 1985). He started his career as an assistant and a professor of Canon Law in Linz, where he also served as Dean of the Faculty of Law (1986 - 1988). Currently he is professor of Canon Law at the *Theologische Fakultät* of the University of Passau (Germany), which Faculty he also served as Dean (1991 - 1993). Since 1976 he is working as an Ecclesiastical Advocate at the Metropolitan Court of Vienna, the Diocesan Courts of Vienna and Linz, and (since 1991) the Courts of Salzburg and Passau. Helmuth Pree is a Member of the *Diocesan Council for the Catholics* in Passau and of the Juridical Commission of the *Verband der Diözesen Deutschlands*.

JAMES H. PROVOST was born in 1939 and is a priest of the Diocese of Helena in the State of Montana, U.S.A. He studied Theology (M.A., S.T.B., Louvain) and Canon Law (J.C.D., Pontifical Lateran University, Rome, 1967). President of the Canon Law Society of America in 1977 and since 1980 managing editor of *The Jurist*, he is professor at the Catholic University of America and currently chairs the Department of Canon Law (since 1987). James H. Provost has published, edited and contributed to several canon law and theological books, including national and international canon law journals. For ten years he served as one of the directors of the church order section of the *International Theological Journal Concilium*.

RIK TORFS was born in 1956. He studied law at Louvain University (lic. iur., 1979; lic. not., 1980) and Canon Law at Strasbourg and Louvain University (J.C.D., 1987). After one year of teaching at Utrecht University (The Netherlands), he became professor at the Faculty of Canon Law (K.U. Leuven) in 1988. Dean of the Faculty of Canon Law since 1993, Rik Torfs published seven books and 150 articles on canon law, law, church and state relationships. He is editor of the *European Journal for Church and State Research*.

Publicaties / Publications Msgr. W. Onclin Chair
Editor Rik Torfs

Canon Law and Marriage. Monsignor W. Onclin Chair 1995, Leuven, Peeters, 1995, 36 p.

R. TORFS, *The Faculty of Canon Law of K.U. Leuven in 1995*, 5-9.
C. BURKE, *Renewal, Personalism and Law*, 11-21.
R.G.W. HUYSMANS, *Enforcement and Deregulation in Canon Law*, 23-36.

A Swing of the Pendulum. Canon Law in Modern Society. Monsignor W. Onclin Chair 1996, Leuven, Peeters, 1996, 64 p.

R. TORFS, *Une messe est possible. Over de nabijheid van Kerk en geloof*, 7-11.
R. TORFS, *'Une messe est possible'. A Challenge for Canon Law*, 13-17.
J.M. SERRANO RUIZ, *Acerca del carácter personal del matrimonio: digresiones y retornos*, 19-31.
J.M. SERRANO RUIZ, *The Personal Character of Marriage. A Swing of the Pendulum*, 33-45.
F.G. MORRISEY, *Catholic Identity of Healthcare Institutions in a Time of Change*, 47-64.